Breathe, Freedom

D1563346

Also by the author:

Beyond Coming Out
Breaking Out
Grade Power
Same-Sex Marriage

Breathe, Freedom

A COMPREHENSIVE AND HYPNOTIC APPROACH TO QUITTING SMOKING

Kevin Alderson, Ph.D.

Registered Psychologist and
Associate Professor of Counselling Psychology
University of Calgary

Editor in Chief
Canadian Journal of Counselling and Psychotherapy

Library and Archives Canada Cataloguing in Publication

Alderson, Kevin, 1956-
         Breathe, freedom! : a comprehensive and hypnotic approach to quitting smoking / Kevin Alderson.

ISBN 978-1-55483-021-3

1. Smoking cessation. 2. Hypnotism--Therapeutic use. 3. Nicotine addiction-- Treatment. I. Title.

HV5740.A44 2011   616.86'506   C2011-900344-9

The publisher gratefully acknowledges the support of the Department of Canadian Heritage through the Book Publishing Industry Development Program.

Printed and bound in Canada

Insomniac Press
520 Princess Avenue,
London, Ontario, Canada, N6B 2B8
www.insomniacpress.com

DEDICATION

A Chilling Forever

"A Forever"
I remember you as a kind gentle soul,
A man who brought smiles when he said hello,
But what you didn't tell me,
And maybe just as well,
Was that when you said goodbye,
You meant it would be forever.

To my late father, George Frederick Alderson

"A Chilling"
I remember seeing you outside on the coldest days,
Huddled in a corner,
Standing alone.
Smoking desperately to breathe,
And breathing desperately to smoke,
Until you could breathe no more.

To my friend Dolores Clarkson

"A Chilling Forever"
I dedicate *Breathe, Freedom* to both of you.
Lung cancer claimed your lives,
But it never claimed your spirits.

Dr. Kevin George Alderson
January 12, 2011

CONTENTS

The Breathe Freedom Stop Smoking Program

PREFACE

I remember being read the occasional fairy tale or fable as a child before falling asleep. Little did I know that these stories contained messages that were actually affecting my moral and spiritual development. There were often themes of good conquers evil, patience pays off, greed will be punished, or some other message that was worth remembering, and interestingly, our minds do remember.

After twenty-nine years of practicing hypnotherapy, I also know that there are those suggestions that are direct, meaning that the intended message is clear, forthright, and obvious. But there are also those suggestions that are indirect, meaning that the intended message is less clear, less forthright, and less obvious. Beyond these types of suggestions are the subliminal ones, the messages that remain ambiguous, hardly perceptible, and/or that appear to be unintentional. There are also those suggestions that perhaps fall into the middle of indirect and subliminal. Their forte is found in metaphor, double entendre, visual imagery, and other such literary devices. I have used all of these types of suggestions in this book.

Comprehensive smoking cessation programs (upon which the non-fictional part of this book is based) boast success rates nearing fifty percent after one year of abstinence. Why isn't the figure higher than that? Recognizing that smoking is an addiction and not merely a habit is part of understanding why this is so. But perhaps another part is recognizing that the most difficult change of all is the one most internal to us: our beliefs. *Metanoia* is a strange word that has several meanings, but the one I prefer to use is that it is a "deep change of mind about something," such as that which occurs when you make a radical change in the way you see the world or the way you view your faith in a higher power.

This book is intended to help create metanoia within you as it relates to your beliefs about your self-worth, your self-confidence, and your life. It is about quitting smoking, and in this, I am committed to providing you the very best of what I know about psychology and hypnotherapy. You might not always know when you are receiving a suggestion about quitting smoking. I hope you find enough fascination with this alone that you will read the entire book right now. After all, you can sleep later, but right now, you might be better off staying awake.

INTRODUCTION

Be prepared to rip this book apart. I mean that literally—you will find it easiest to rip out the pages from the second part of this book to work with the material. Although the complete Breathe Freedom Stop Smoking Program is contained there, do not jump to it before reading the story of Freedom, a shy lonely boy who goes through significant trauma in getting through adolescence and coming to terms with what is really important in life.

Feel free also to rip this book apart figuratively. The Breathe Freedom program is based on my review of five thousand journal article abstracts from 1967 to the present, and a careful reading of nearly a hundred of the most important published articles found in the psychological literature and several current books. Besides this, I have been a licensed psychologist for twenty-five years and I have practiced hypnotherapy since 1982. I have helped hundreds of smokers to quit. Perhaps it is now your time to do the same.

This book does not use scare tactics, unlike many other books that overemphasize the harm caused by cigarettes. You already know much of this, but for a quick reminder, smoking is the number one preventable cause of disease in the world, and that includes Canada, the U.S., Britain, Europe, and Australia.

Researchers have found about four thousand chemicals in cigarette smoke, and of these, over forty are known to cause cancer (McEwen et al., 2006). The three most important components include:

1. *nicotine*, which is the drug that keeps smokers smoking; however, it does not itself cause cancer,
2. *tar*, and this substance is linked to cancer, lung disease, heart disease, and certain other smoking-related diseases, and
3. *carbon monoxide*, which is a gas emitted from cigarettes that is linked to heart disease and adverse effects during pregnancy.

Long-term smokers who don't quit will lose, on average, ten years of life. Between a half to two-thirds of long-term smokers will lose more than that—about twenty years compared to those who never smoked. Their deaths will be mainly attributable to cancer, cardiovascular disease, and lung disease. Smokers have a fifteen times greater chance of developing lung cancer and twice the chance of developing heart disease because of continued smoking (McEwen et al., 2006).

Approximately twenty to twenty-three percent of adults in Canada, the U.S., Australia, and Britain smoke (Gorin and Schnoll, 2006; Richmond, 2006; Waldroup, Gifford, and Kalra, 2006). According to the American Lung

Association, it is the leading cause of death in the U.S. Statistics from 2006 revealed that tobacco use caused approximately 440,000 deaths per year in the U.S (George, 2007). In 2010, an estimated 222,520 Americans will develop lung cancer (American Cancer Society, 2010). The leading cause: smoking cigarettes. The situation is no different in Canada, where according to the Canadian Cancer Society, approximately 24,200 Canadians will be diagnosed with lung cancer in 2010, and today it remains the leading cause of death in both men and women (Canadian Cancer Society, 2010).

Throughout the world, more men smoke compared to women. Globally, approximately forty-eight percent of men and twelve percent of women smoke, which is about 1.1 billion smokers. By 2025, the number is expected to rise to more than 1.6 billion (Richmond, 2006). Although smoking rates are diminishing in developed countries, it continues to rise in underdeveloped ones and in Asia. For example, the prevalence of smoking among males in Asian countries is shockingly high: forty-five percent in India, fifty-three percent in Japan, sixty-three percent in China, sixty-nine percent in Indonesia, and seventy-three percent in Vietnam (Edwards, 2004).

Even by age twenty, the vast majority (i.e., about eighty percent) of smokers regret that they ever started, but their addiction will rule much of their adult lives (Jarvis, 2004). Like most other drug addictions, smoking is known for its high relapse rates. The successful quitter has tried to quit smoking on average six times (Richmond and Zwar, 2003).

Each year, about forty percent of smokers in the U.S.

attempt to quit, and although most smokers prefer to quit on their own, less than ten percent will be successful after a one-year follow-up period (Sarna and Bialous, 2006; Richmond and Zwar, 2003). Comprehensive smoking cessation programs, like the one this book describes, boast success rates that approach fifty percent after one year (Elkins and Rajab, 2004; Hatsukami and Mooney, 1999; Shadel and Shiffman, 2005).

The good news is that the benefits of quitting smoking begin right *now!* The lungs begin to clear out cigarette debris, including mucus, within twenty-four hours. The body eliminates carbon monoxide within forty-eight hours, and smell and taste begin to improve. Breathing becomes easier and energy increases within seventy-two hours. Circulation improves between two and twelve weeks, and coughing and wheezing diminish significantly between three and nine months. The risk of heart attack reduces to half of that of a smoker in a year, and by ten years, the risk of contracting lung cancer becomes half of that of a smoker. After fifteen years, the risk of heart attack becomes about the same as someone who has never smoked (McEwen et al., 2006).

Is it *your* time to stop smoking? You already know the answer to this. Read on and find out for yourself how easy it is to make this happen once and for all.

References

American Cancer Society. 2010. *Cancer facts and figures 2010*. http://www.cancer.org/Research/CancerFacts Figures/CancerFactsFigures/cancer-facts-and-figures-2010

Canadian Cancer Society. 2010. *Lung cancer statistics*. http://www.cancer.ca/Canada-wide/About%20cancer/ Cancer%20statistics/Stats%20at%20a%20glance/Lung %20cancer.aspx?sc_lang=en

Edwards, R. 2004. ABC of smoking cessation: The problem of tobacco smoking. *BMJ: British Medical Journal*, 328(7433):217–19.

Elkins, G. R., and Rajab, M. H. 2004. Clinical hypnosis for smoking cessation: Preliminary results of a three-session intervention. *International Journal of Clinical and Experimental Hypnosis*, 52(1):73–81.

George, T. P., ed. 2007. *Medication treatments for nicotine dependence*. Boca Raton, FL: CRC Press.

Gorin, S. S., and Schnoll, R. A. 2006. Smoking cessation. In S. S. Gorin and J. Arnold, eds., *Health promotion in practice*. San Francisco, CA: Jossey-Bass, 287-328.

Hatsukami, D. K., and Mooney, M. E. 1999. Pharmacological and behavioral strategies for smoking cessation. *Journal of Clinical Psychology in Medical Settings*, 6(1):11–38.

Jarvis, M. J. 2004. ABC of smoking cessation: Why people smoke. *BMJ: British Medical Journal*, 328(7434):277–79.

McEwen, A., et al. 2006. *Manual of smoking cessation: A guide for counsellors and practitioners*. Malden, MA: Blackwell.

Richmond, R. 2006. Reflections on smoking cessation research. *Drug and Alcohol Review*, 25(1):1–3.

Richmond, R., and Zwar, N. 2003. Review of bupropion for smoking cessation. *Drug and Alcohol Review*,

22(2):203–20.

Sarna, L., and Bialous, S. A. 2006. Strategic directions for nursing research in tobacco dependence. *Nursing Research*, 55(4, Suppl):S1–S9.

Shadel, W. G., and Shiffman, S. 2005. Assessment of smoking behavior. In D. M. Donovan and G. A. Marlatt, eds., *Assessment of addictive behaviors* (2nd ed.) New York: Guilford Press, 113–54.

Waldroup, W. M., Gifford, E. V., and Kalra, P. 2006. Adherence to smoking cessation treatments. In W. T. O'Donohue and E. R. Levensky, eds., *Promoting treatment adherence: A practical handbook for health care providers*. Thousand Oaks, CA: Sage, 235–52.

Chapter 1
THE BEGINNINGS OF CONFLICT

This wasn't the first time I spent several hours on Wreck Beach. For those unfamiliar with this remarkable place, Wreck Beach is Canada's largest clothing-optional beach, and you find it by taking Trail #6 down to the ocean's edge from the University of British Columbia campus in Vancouver.

I wouldn't want you to think that this is "my scene" or anything like that, however. Frankly, while I was growing up, I never really understood what this place represented to the regulars or to my parents for that matter. Well, until now, that is. At age forty-two, a lot more things make sense in my life.

I had forgotten what it feels like to get naked and perch exposed skin on a well-worn log, being careful not to take in any slivers. Slivers hurt, especially when they stab you where the sun doesn't shine. I've found a good spot, though, where I can sit for the next few hours and tell you my story. I'll share with you a little about my background before re-membering what it was like for me as a thirteen-year-old, which is when my life really started to evolve.

My parents had made excursions to Wreck Beach a

regular summer pastime, and I was forced to tag along. God, how many times did I have to see naked people flopping themselves around in front of me? I figure "clothing optional" should mean "show a little respect." But my parents had to make it a point to bare all, and they forced me to do the same. I remember hating to be with them in this altered state. You would think I should be used to it, and indeed, I should be used to it. I suppose we all find ways to rebel against our parents at some point, and in hindsight, I wished it only went as far as my parents. However, I will tell you about that later.

I have started to embrace some of what I discarded long ago—my name, for instance. My name is Freedom, by the way, and it is a pleasure to meet you. If it weren't for hippie parents, I suspect I would have had a more common name like most normal people. I always thought I looked more like a Roger. *Roger this*, and *Roger that*—a complacent shy boy who aimed to please. Like so many seasons in a person's life, however, that changed eventually, and I can credit my name with much of this transformation. Before I forget to mention, I have a younger sister. Her name is Star. I usually call her *pathetic*, but she also has names for me I won't mention here. We're even, I figure.

Without my name, there would be no story—well, at least not this one. Let me give you some idea of my upbringing. I was born and raised at a time when "make love, not war" was the motto of a people conflicted by their nation's torn beliefs, along with the controversial actions they took. It seems to me that nearly all actions are controversial, including that of my parents.

My parents rebelled, and when they could, they left the sanctuary of their commune near San Francisco and we moved to Vancouver. That was in May 1971, and I was already an anxious preschooler, waiting nervously to begin kindergarten in September. My dad was a great support, though. My favourite memories of kindergarten were the times he spent with me. He had more time than most dads, and what I didn't realize then was why. Simply put, he had trouble finding and keeping work. Instead of working, he would take me down to the beach and we would laugh our heads off at the stupidest things. We threw Frisbees, he chased me and wrestled with me, and we ate ice cream (lots of ice cream) and other sweets. I'd have to say that Dad had a sweeter tooth than I did!

Dad always looked tired, but that is only because his eyes were forever red and bloodshot. He always had a permanent smile on his face, however, and I interpreted that to mean he was really happy. I didn't know the real reasons for this at the time, and back then, I didn't care. I was loved, and that is all that mattered for a child.

Dad didn't seem that smart though—he was often forgetful. One year he even forgot my birthday but made up for it with lots of kisses, hugs, and just appreciation for who I am. A few toys followed, but never very many. My family didn't have much money at all.

I really loved my mom too. She had really long black hair, and sometimes she had it braided. She always wore these dresses or sarongs made of natural fibers, and when standing, she looked amazingly beautiful. Mom often seemed preoccupied with her own stuff and teaching Star how to do domestic things. One time Star decided to cook an entire meal herself, and Mom let her. I wanted to regurgitate every bite, but I knew I couldn't without getting punished. I hoped Star never cooked again.

My parents were often smoking, not only the regular cigarettes but also the sweet smelling tobacco from the "octopus." That's what I called their pipe because it had six hoses sticking out of it.

I hated the way their cigarettes smelled and the way it made me cough when too much secondhand smoke got the better of me. Driving in the car with the windows closed seemed like the worst experience, but even that I got used to eventually.

What I never got used to were the times my parents' friends visited us. One or two other couples would come over and they would all smoke from the octopus. Sometimes they would all get naked, and that's usually when Star and I would go downstairs to get away. Man, I didn't know why they have to take off their clothes like that. I knew I could never have any friends come over for fear my parents would be "inappropriate." God, why was it the kid who had to be the responsible one? It didn't help that I already felt different from other kids. Why? Because I am shy, quiet, and embarrassed by my parents. I already felt this way at age five.

Kindergarten itself was actually fun, so my anxiousness was soon put to rest. Sometimes, however, other kids laughed at my name. I didn't usually mind because I could laugh with them. Grade school was a different experience altogether, however. I was constantly teased because of my stupid name. I didn't make any friends and I felt isolated and strange. I remained embarrassed to bring anyone over, and because of this, I only did once during my growing years.

The bullying began innocently enough, I suppose. Name-calling was the start of it. It's amazing how many ways a name can be altered, and a simple name such as Freedom became "Bleedom," "Seedum," "Needham," and "Eat-um." But it progressed from there. Some bullies would add actions to the name-calling, so after calling me Needham, they would try to knee me, or they would call me Eat-um while trying to bite me as they continued their stupid chant. The more I told them to stop it, the more it seemed to egg them on. I was afraid to tell teachers or anyone else at school about this for fear it would only get worse. When someone at the school did see me being bullied, he or she would tell the kids to stop it and move on, but that only ended it temporarily. Next opportunity they got, the bullying returned.

I told my parents about it. Mom suggested I tell the principal and Dad suggested I work harder at becoming their friend. One thing I liked then about my parents is that they never intervened for me; instead, they believed that even children ought to take care of their own fights and take responsible steps to get through a situation. Their suggestions were suggestions, and I would be the one that had to act upon them if I chose.

As an adult, I accept that life is like that. No one else can live my life other than me. In retrospect, however, I think parents need to stand up for their children, especially when they can't get through something on their own. They also need to be role models to their children, and my parents didn't do a good job of that in many areas.

Anyway, I didn't choose either action. Telling the principal was out of the question, as I was sure it would lead to worse bullying. Becoming friends with these bullies did not seem possible either. I mean, really, how would that look? Was I supposed to kiss their behinds while they continued picking on me? I didn't think so, so I ignored them as best I could. I figured that by junior high, this treatment would end. Eventually kids mature, and I thought I would have to wait this one out until they did.

I am maturing too. I'm about to turn thirteen and begin grade seven. Three elementary schools feed this junior high, and I am delighted to see so many unfamiliar faces. A fresh start, and I breathe a sigh of relief. Unfortunately, there are also familiar faces, and when they see me, the name-calling begins once again. A few weeks go by and I ask myself, "How many times can a kid get pushed into the lockers?" The answer is, "As many times as they—the bullies—feel like."

By junior high school, you would think I would be used to being bullied, and I am. Over time, I have simply come to believe that I deserve this treatment. However, there are three bullies who have come from a different feeder school and I don't know how to deal with them. Their aggression towards me is escalating, and not only am I getting pushed into lockers and bumped for no good reason as they walk by, but they are also into punching me in the stomach, ripping my shirt, and throwing me to the ground.

These three guys form a gang, and I have never encountered gang behaviour before. Their names are Shane, Mike, and Cory. They always dress exactly alike: baggy blue jeans that nearly fall off their waists; runners; backwards baseball caps; and skintight, white, tank-top undershirts when inside school and shirtless when outside. A big part of me is envious because I have never belonged to any peer group, let alone a cool-looking gang like this one. Nonetheless, they're not looking at me as their friend—and I'm not looking at them as mine either.

It's Halloween 1979, and as I leave school for the day, I soon realize fright night is starting early. I am a few blocks away from the school when I see the shirtless gang in front of me. I cringe inside, my nerves melting as I stare at their smirks.

Shane speaks first, "Well, freak, you're right on time. We've noticed that sometimes you're here at five after four, but other times at five to four. You aren't very consistent really, are you? It doesn't matter because it's time we teach you a lesson."

I plead, "Why do you guys keep this going? I haven't done anything to any of you. Please leave me alone and stop this."

Cory, now glistening with sweat and looking angry, retorts, "You freak, we will never leave you alone. You deserve exactly what we are about to give you." With that, he punches me hard in the gut, and before I can crunch over, he brings his knee up into my groin. I fall to the ground while the three of them begin kicking me, being careful to miss my head to avoid leaving any marks.

The few minutes feels like hours, and after they leave, I lay there awhile to collect my thoughts. The beating was actually quite mild, but it's the first time I have ever been assaulted outside the confines of school. Plus, I don't know how much worse things might get over the ensuing months.

I really wanted to talk to my parents when I got home, but they are both baked and far too high to talk intelligibly. Maybe tomorrow will be better, I don't know. I have begun to learn that our minds are capable of the greatest degrees of denial, because even a few hours later, I am convincing myself that it probably won't happen again. Maybe my parents are in denial too, of their smoking of both pot and cigarettes. Maybe they don't realize how screwed up they are, or how they are hurting themselves. I figure it would sure be nice to see Dad hold down a decent job for more than a week or two. It's not going to happen, I guess, as he probably prefers instead to hide from reality and live his dope-smoking life. God, it makes me angry at times, but I have my own crap to deal with. Anyway, I soon forget about the beating and carry on at school as though nothing happened.

Denial is really about not facing up to the stuff in our life that is real; however, sooner or later, it either breaks on its own or another dose of reality hits and you wake up once again, even if only for a moment. November 28 is one of those days. Again, I have left school and I am but a few blocks from home when out of my peripheral vision, I see Mike motioning his friends to come out of hiding behind some bushes. This time, the three of them are wearing hoodies, as the temperature and light rain is cool. I also feel a coldness and dampness of spirit strike as I realize my denial has broken. I'm hoping it's only my denial that breaks as the three approach me.

Cory grabs me from behind while Mike says, "Welcome back, freak. Wrestle all you want, but you aren't free, are you? Mikey is sure happy to see you out here again though." With that, he undoes my jacket and shirt, and then focuses his punch right above my navel before delivering it. He punches me a second and third time before pausing to see my reaction. I wince in pain, but I do not say a word. Neither does he as he motions for Cory to throw me to the ground. The three of them again start kicking me, and the minutes are longer this time before they stop and run away. This time, my stomach feels a bit bruised, and perhaps my left leg as well. I don't want to think about this right now, but this incident has registered within me more than the first time it happened, and a part of me knows I will need to do something about it. I am scared, but I don't want to feel what grips me inside. I try to forget what just happened, but this time, anxious thoughts intrude my consciousness, leaving me feeling vulnerable and weak. I don't like this feeling.

Perhaps it is coincidence or just plain luck, but that evening Dad turns on a movie he had seen a few years ago at a theatre. It's called *Billy Jack*.

Dad says, "I want you and Star to watch this movie with your Mom and me. It helps portray some of the things we believe in."

I guess having a family night might be okay, so I sit

down, and we watch the show. My God, this movie is having an impact on me more than I would have expected! Tom Laughlin stars as Billy Jack, and he is a freedom fighter.

I ask, "What is this form of fighting called, Dad?"

"I believe it is hapkido or something like that, Freedom."

I register that—I'm thinking, this is what I need to learn! I need to learn to kick the crap out of these bullies, and the sooner the better.

Okay, I know school personnel won't agree with me, but sometimes talk isn't enough. To deal with these bullies, I decide I need to learn a martial art. I look through the phone book and find a studio that looks appealing and is also close to where I live. Luckily, I find one that is not far off the route I take to get home from school. It's called Hiro's Aikido Dojo.

The next day, I decide to check it out after school. I walk into the studio a few minutes before 4 p.m. and a class is about to begin. A middle-aged Japanese man wearing a black belt approaches me and asks if I want to observe the class.

"Yes please," I say.

"Sit down there. Be quiet, and sit," he replies.

Although he speaks in a soft tone, I know he means business. I sit, and I don't make a sound. I am afraid to breathe, in fact. I watch spellbound as kids younger than me throw each other around like tops. As I watch one attacker go down after another, I know I have found the right place. Some of the moves look incredible, and that is what I want; this is what I need to learn. I am ready to become a devastating nemesis. Let those bullies come and get me after a few quick lessons!

After the class ends, the Japanese instructor motions for me to come over to his desk in the corner of the studio. "*Stop!*" he yells at me as I begin to traipse across the wall-to-wall mat. I nearly fall over I am so stunned by the authority I hear in his voice. He says, "Take off shoes and socks before proceed further."

Of course, I'm realizing, everyone on the mat I saw earlier was barefoot, and obviously I am expected to do the same. Sometimes I feel so stupid. I don't know how I have survived even this far.

He stands up as I get close, bows, and stares at me with anticipation. I get it, and I bow in the same way he did to me. He says, "Sit down. We talk." After we sit, he continues, "My name is Sensei Hiro, and you have entered my dojo. Tell me what bring you here."

I later learn that *dojo* simply means "training studio" or "facility." For now, I reply with, "My name is Freedom. I'm being constantly bullied and beat up because of my name. Actually, I'm beginning to think it's happening because of who I am. I don't belong, and this is hurting me more than the beatings I take. I want to learn how to defend myself."

"Then you call me *Sensei*, Freedom," he says, "and you start tomorrow."

He can see my mouth drop as I am thrown off by his immediacy. He who I must now call Sensei continues, "You ready to learn aikido, yes?"

"Yes, I am ready, Sensei."

"Then start tomorrow. Don't worry about getting uniform yet. You buy after we see if this work for us."

"What should I wear then?" I ask.

"Wear comfortable for you."

"What about cost?"

"There no cost for you now, Freedom. We need to know if this right for you first. Come tomorrow afternoon at ten to four. Change in locker room, and leave your clothes, shoes, and socks there." He points to the opposite corner. "As you approach mat, bow, then sit quietly."

"Thank you, Sensei. I will do as you say."

I leave there and I feel like a million dollars! I'm literally jumping up and down as I run home. Strangely, it's not because I will be learning how to fight the bullies. No, it's more because Sensei has accepted me! He made me feel like it would be the greatest honour to study and learn from him. Somehow, through his mannerisms, I pick up some of his incredible strength and knowledge. Strength and knowledge—that seems especially meaningful to me right now. Right now. That seems especially meaningful to me right now.

I get home and tell my parents about my intention to begin aikido tomorrow. They completely disagree. I should have expected this. They are both pacifists, and I swear, the worst violence they ever saw was someone thrashing around on a bad LSD trip. I ask my parents if they ever tried LSD and Mom gives me the politically correct answer: "Freedom, those were different times, and people acted in a way that made sense to them then."

Nuff said. I now know they used it, and maybe they used it a lot. I'd always thought that Star was a genetic mutation, but I've changed my view since becoming a teenager. Now I simply see her as a biological experiment gone wrong. In all seriousness, she is okay, but she is my sis and I am entitled to tease her.

I decided I needed to go against my parents' wishes. That is difficult for me because I try really hard to please, but honestly, they never give me good advice about anything. If they had their way, I'd just put up with all the crap I get dished because I am supposed to be a pacifist too. I don't buy that philosophy! If they were the ones who were constantly being harassed, I'm sure they wouldn't be waiting passively around for the next abuser to appear.

I will soon be fighting the crap out of these bullies. I swear, they are going to take one hell of a beating!

Chapter 2

FIGHTING BACK

The alarm wakes me at 7 a.m. and I grudgingly get out of bed. Before leaving, I nearly forget that I need to bring some clothes to wear during the aikido class. I pack up some jogging pants and a white tank top before heading to school. The entire day, I think about getting started in aikido. Talk about gnawing at the bit! I was out the door the moment the bell rang at 3:30 p.m. Even the bullies wouldn't have been able to keep up to me today. I arrive at the dojo at 3:45 p.m., change, sit down, and wait. A kid beside me looks to be about eleven years old and is wearing a white belt. I say, "Hello, my name is Freedom. Are you also new to aikido?"

"Hi, Freedom. I'm Chris," he replies. "This is my third year of aikido actually." When he sees my surprised look, he continues, "No one here gets coloured belts until they are ready to test for a black belt. This is a common practice in aikido, although I know there are some schools that give coloured belts before black."

"How close are you to getting a black belt?"

"I will be testing in June or so—soon after my thirteenth birthday. Do you know that Sensei has a ninth *dan*, also known as *kyudan*?"

I am about to respond and ask Chris another question when Sensei enters. Everyone stops talking. We stand, bow, and sit down again. Not a sound is uttered and I am frankly afraid to even burp. Sensei notices my presence and acknowledges me with a slight head nod. He then immediately moves to instructing the class.

After a few demonstrations, Sensei tells us to pick someone to practice these moves called immobilizations. I am relieved that Chris picks me to be his partner. For the next hour, I feel like we are dancing as I begin to learn that aikido is about making many circular motions to redirect the energy of attackers and to ultimately neutralize their attack. It's kind of like taking the wind out of their sails. After class, I change and leave for home.

The class meets Mondays, Wednesdays, and Fridays, and it is clear that many absences are not tolerated.

After two weeks of attending faithfully, Sensei nods for me to see him after class. "Freedom, you have good spirit. I accept you into class. You want to be my student?"

"Yes, Sensei, this is what I need!"

"Then time for you to wear *gi*, and lessons cost twenty dollars a month."

"Thank you. I will bring you the money next class."

As I'm leaving, I begin thinking about how I am going to earn the money to afford this! God, I should have thought about this sooner. My only choice right now is to ask my parents for the money, but seeing that neither of them agree with martial arts training and Dad is again unemployed, I'm not optimistic.

When I get home, I sheepishly make my plea. "Dad, I need to borrow fifty dollars from you."

"What do you need it for, Freedom?"

"I need to pay for my first month of aikido and buy a uniform."

"I don't have fifty dollars. I haven't been working for a couple of weeks," he says.

I feel my blood begin to boil as I exclaim, "Maybe if you weren't baked most of the day, someone would hire you!"

Okay, that was the wrong thing to say, and sure enough, Dad replies, "My problems finding work have nothing to do with my use of pot, Freedom, and you are out of line. Good luck in finding the money to feed your violent sport."

Okay, calm down, do not retaliate. There is no point making the situation even worse. I storm from the house to collect my thoughts and think about my next step. Where am I going to get the money? I am so angry that my dad is the loser that he is. Any other kid could get money from their parents, but not me. Man, I begin thinking about every possible way to make some cash quickly. Rob a bank? Sell my body on the street? Push drugs? Desperation creates desperate thoughts. I eventually get a grip and push desperation aside. I will not live a desperate life, now or ever. I refuse to live a desperate life.

"Breathe," I tell myself. "Just breathe, Freedom. I'll find a job."

I decide to skip school the next day to begin looking for a part-time job—my first job! I'm not sure how much my age will be a barrier, but I have a determined spirit. I have probably gone to fifteen places before someone bites. An older woman at Shoppers Drug Mart reaches over and says, "I need someone to stock shelves on Saturdays. Are you interested?"

Nearly jumping for joy, I belch out, "Absolutely! How much will I get paid?"

"Three dollars an hour to start. If you work out well, I'll give you a raise in three months."

I gratefully accept. According to my calculations, I should earn about $80 a month or so, which is even more than I need. The problem is, what do I do about getting my uniform before I get paid, and how will I pay Sensei for the first month? I decide to wait until tomorrow's class to ask Sensei about this, hoping he will understand.

After class on Friday, I approach Sensei, bow, and ask if I may speak to him. He invites me to his desk in the corner.

"Sensei, I have no money, and neither do my parents. My father is a slob and he doesn't work half the time. I got a job that I begin on Saturday, and I will have money for you in a month. Is that okay?"

"No, it is *not* okay! It is not okay way you speak about father, that is," scolds Sensei. "You must show father respect, as we show friends and enemies."

I am confused by his answer, so I remain silent and listen, expressing confusion through my facial expressions.

"You see, Freedom, there is no freedom in hate or violence—one causes other. Only through path called respect can you learn to move mountains out of way."

"Sensei, may I stay in your class without any money this month?" I sputter as I get worried I may not be allowed to continue.

"Freedom, not need to ask—of course. When I welcomed you, no conditions—no money back either once you pay. Give me minute and I return." Sensei leaves for his back room, and when he returns, he is carrying a white uniform with him and a white belt. "Wear this, Freedom."

I thank him and head home for the weekend.

By March, I am ready to get tested for fifth *kyū*. *Kyū* is the category of rank in my school that denotes the level of white belt before reaching black belt, at which point rank is measured by *dan*. All students of aikido begin at the level of sixth *kyū*, which is another way of saying beginner, I suppose. Over time, beginners move up the ranks in reverse order until they have achieved first *kyū*. After that, they begin moving up the ranks of *dan* (black belt) in ascending order. The highest level of black belt is *jyudan* (tenth degree), but it is rumoured that only one aikido expert ever reached that level.

Anyway, I demonstrate my ability to execute some basic techniques, and Sensei tells me I have passed the test for fifth *kyū*. I am honoured, but I am also frustrated.

"Sensei, for the past three months, I have practiced several methods to neutralize an enemy by bringing them down to the ground and by diverting their attack away from me. When do I learn to kick the crap out of one or more enemies?" I ask.

Sensei's bottom lip begins to curl, which I've learned means that I am about to hear a lesson. He begins, "Freedom, self-defense is not at peril of someone else. It is in loving enemy that we find the peace that aikido known for." Sensei notices I am becoming agitated and pipes in,

"Beating someone not what we do. Instead, we show respect while protect ourselves from ill-intentioned attack."

I am beginning to lose it, and my face turns red. God, Sensei is beginning to sound like my parents, and I blurt out, "Then *what the hell am I doing here?!* I need to learn to kick and punch hard!"

Sensei is amazing. I never see him lose his cool as I just did. Instead, his lip curls more than normal and he says, "Freedom, go home now. Come back Monday. You are baby in crib, not understand art form yet."

My face turns even redder now, but I have learned respect for Sensei and I oblige, realizing I may have wasted the past few months learning this crap. I didn't think there was much difference between this and what I saw Billy Jack doing. I keep telling myself I need to learn how to punch and kick.

It's not like the bullying has stopped, by the way. The situation at school hasn't changed, although it's only a handful of guys who continue pushing me into lockers now. Some who used to bully me seem to have now found different interests, meaning different targets. Bullies are bullies, and victims are victims. I'm not sure that will ever change. Sensei seems to have a different philosophy, and it's just as stupid as my parents' views on war, fighting, killing, and the like. I am a sitting duck for another attack, and I'm not sure what to do about it right now. I decide that I will continue my lessons in aikido, at least until school year ends.

It's finally June and school will finish in three weeks. I will also be tested for my fourth *kyū* in another ten days. We get some exceptional days in Vancouver in the summer time, and this is one of them. It's a particularly hot day, the temperature sitting at nearly 28 degrees Celsius (82 degrees Fahrenheit). I like to wear cut offs and flip-flops to school on days like this, together with a light tank top. I'm feeling a light perspiration on my skin as I head for aikido class. The air gets still heavier as my intuition screams that someone is following me. I look behind me, but I don't see anyone. All of that changes within minutes, however.

"*You freak!*" I hear as I again turn around, but before I can prepare a defensive response, I am being grabbed in front by the throat. As I struggle to shake off Shane's chokehold, Mike locks me into a full nelson. Shane then rips my tank top in half and tears it off me, throwing it to the side. I'm feeling Mike's sweaty chest against my back, and I am trying my best to throw him off of me, but I cannot budge. Shane moves in and begins a barrage of punches to my gut and my chest, leaving huge red marks wherever he connects. Cory is watching, calling me all kinds of names while I begin sinking to the ground. I actually don't remember the next few minutes. In fact, I don't remember anything until I vaguely see a figure coming into focus that looks like Chris.

It is Chris, and he helps me to my feet. My body hurts this time, and I am in no shape to go to aikido. Chris realizes this and says, "Freedom, I don't know what just happened. I found you here like this a few minutes ago. Do you know your attackers?"

I struggle to respond for a few moments before spitting out, "Yes, I know them. They are the reason I started aikido. I was unable to defend myself against them, and their attacks are getting worse. I don't know what to do, Chris. There are three of them."

"Listen—let me help you home and I'll tell Sensei what happened. He'll know what to do."

We get to my place and as I open the door, the smell of burning weed and cigarettes is nearly overpowering. Chris smells it too, but he doesn't say a word about it.

I introduce him to my stoner parents, and without further ado, I say, "Thanks for helping me, Chris. See you on Monday at aikido."

"My pleasure, Freedom. Have a good weekend."

That night, my mom answers the phone and tells me I have a call. Now that's different— no one ever calls me. Am I in trouble for something?

The affirming Japanese voice is unmistakable. "Freedom, I hear what happen. Come to dojo now. We talk."

"Thank you, Sensei. I'll be there in fifteen minutes."

I arrive, remove my flip-flops, bow, and traverse the mat to where Sensei is seated. He rises, and we both bow.

"Sit down. Chris told me what happen. You okay?"

I hesitate. "Yes…I'm okay…Sensei."

"You no okay, Freedom. I hear sound of fear, anger. You must release this so spirit can sing once more. Your spirit can sing once more. Freedom, you not be controlled by emotion. You must conquer fear inside—no place for it. No place for fear anymore. I know you tell me you picked on by other kids, but you not share extent of this suffering. You are most shy indeed. Why not mom and dad help?"

Tears swell in my eyes, and I whisper, "My dad is stupid. Sorry, that is not what I mean. My dad is ill. He is weak, and he smokes too many cigarettes and too much marijuana."

"I see. You keep many things inside, Freedom. I make offer for you."

My eyes perk up. "What do you wish to offer me, Sensei?"

"School soon out. You come here every morning at nine until five, like job. You take more classes here, you clean dojo, like job. For this, you pay no money for classes in July and August. I teach you deal with attack from three—again, immobilize, project, subdue enemy. Not to hurt enemy, I do not teach you."

Crying like a baby is not something I am proud of. I would rather be gagged with a pacifier, quite honestly. With a gurgling noise, I reply, "Yes, Sensei, I would like that."

"Good. Begin July first, not July second. You also here July fourth, no exception. You here to learn, not indulge." I nod and leave behind a part of my heart in Sensei's soul.

The summer becomes a fountain of learning. My only regret is not having more one-on-one time with Sensei. He is a man of few words to begin with, but I am always riveted by the words he does say. His words capture my attention, for I am beginning to understand some of the wisdom upon which such words are built.

At the end of August, after going through many repetitions of basic and advanced moves, Sensei speaks, "Freedom, you test for first *kyū* one week today."

I turn fourteen on September 20, and I can't believe that I may be one step away from getting my first *dan*! Over the next week, I practice my moves as often as I can—at the dojo, at home, before school, after school, whenever and wherever.

I breeze through my test for first *kyū*. The black belts watching smile as Sensei tells me I have passed.

Soon summer passes too, and school is back in full swing. The air is still hot and humid on September 19, a day before my birthday. I don't know why I now sometimes feel the premonition of something before it happens. Perhaps intuition is something that comes from training or from getting older. I don't know, but trouble is oozing through the gentle wind that tries unsuccessfully to tangle my wavy hair. Perhaps I am stronger than the wind. Perhaps I am stronger than I know.

I look for Cory, Mike, and Shane. I know today they are out here, waiting for me like a vulture waits for death. However, I find the peace inside that Sensei taught me. I feel no fear, no doubt, and no anger. I only feel focus. I breathe, and I feel focus.

The three sweaty shirtless dudes soon stand before me, each smirking in their demented way. As they advance toward me, I feel as though the world is now moving in slow motion. My body begins to move without my conscious deliberations. Instead, I begin to move gracefully, the dance that Sensei would appreciate as an expression of the harmony of inner centralization and sphericity (i.e. circular movements).

As they lash out their aggressions, I deliberately redirect, channel, and project their force, neutralizing each attack and each one of them. As they begin falling over each other and hitting one another inadvertently, they become increasingly dazed and confused. Before long, each one is panting on the ground, shaking off cobwebs that represent a far cry from what they experienced with me last Halloween.

I never knew this, but Shane is their leader. He stands up first, shaking the dirt off his jeans and picking off debris from his bare torso, before speaking. "That was amazing. I have never seen anyone move like that before. Where did you learn to fight like this?"

"It doesn't matter. What matters is that I'm no longer going to put up with this abuse," I proclaim confidently.

Shane replies apologetically, "We were wrong to treat you like this. Obviously, we completely underestimated you."

"Maybe you did."

After talking awhile, I begin feeling disquieted as I hear Shane utter the unexpected. "Freedom, I want you to join our gang. You belong with us."

Belong? The word resonates in my head. "Did I hear you correctly, Shane?"

"Yes, you heard me. I want you in our gang."

Man, I can't believe this is happening! Despite their bullying, I have always thought these guys were the coolest. Each one has well-defined muscles, and I love their uniform! Now I don't believe in giving immediate answers to important questions, so I wait half a minute before stating, "*Yes I want to belong!*"

"Good choice, Freedom." Shane smiles. "Belonging is

only dependent upon one thing…. You must pass our initiation."

My gulp hides neither my excitement nor my trepidation. "What do you mean…initiation?" I cringe inside as I stammer slightly.

"All members of a gang must prove themselves. It's how one demonstrates their worthiness, right guys?" he asks of Mike and Cory. Both nod, and Shane continues, "You have nothing to worry about, Freedom. With your moves, you will easily pass the necessary rite of passage."

"What am I expected to do, Shane?" It feels like jagged knives are sliding down my throat as I breathe heavily. "What will initiation look like?"

Chapter 3

BELONGING

"The first and most important part of your initiation means winning a battle against one of our rivals," Shane explains. "Our gang has been in conflict with the Tonner boys since we became organized two years ago. Your job will be to fight Mark Tonner, the second eldest of the four brothers. He's in grade nine at a school near the west end. Do not underestimate him. He's tough to the bone, five foot ten, and one hundred and sixty pounds of solid muscle. You must win the fight to belong to our gang."

Part of my heart sinks as the implication of this settles deeper into my mind. "I need two days to think about it. I will let you know after my birthday," I answer.

"Okay, you have two days to decide. Let me write down your phone number. I'll call you in exactly two days."

I tell him my number as I begin walking away. I feel a sickening conflict wrestling within me already. Fight and belong, or decline and continue to feel isolated? Fighting would also go against Sensei's teachings about generating respect and peaceful relations with others. Hmm—maybe I will have some clarity about this after my birthday.

As it turns out, my birthday is a huge disappointment. Dad had said he wanted to spend time with me, yet he is still asleep at 3 p.m. By the time he showers and has breakfast, it's nearly four. I look at his all-too-familiar bloodshot eyes and my blood begins to boil. "Why the hell are you getting up so late in the day?!" I shout. "It's my birthday, and even celebrating this is too much effort for you!"

It strikes me that there is something backwards about this. Isn't it the parent who is supposed to be coming down on their teenage kids instead of the reverse? Anyway, Dad does muster a reply.

"Freedom, it's not your job to tell me what I should or shouldn't do. It's time you show a little respect."

Respect? Why should I show my dad respect? I know Sensei's thoughts about this, but he doesn't have to live in this wasteland of a family. "I'm going out to get some fresh air. I'll be home in a while."

Dad doesn't answer back.

The walk provides me the opportunity to do some serious soul searching. I begin to think that although Sensei is wise, he is out of touch with the reality of teens my age. The fact is, we live in a win-or-lose world, and I know which end of the equation I want to be on. Sensei's teachings are well-intentioned, but they don't always apply.

I *really* want to belong to this gang. I've noticed the hot babes that swoon over these guys, and maybe I can attract one or two myself. I am fourteen now after all, and my hormones are making *me* moan more often than I care to admit. Perhaps I can finally get laid! Wow, and maybe even get a girlfriend!

My mind is settled. When Shane calls me, I tell him I want in. He tells me where to buy my new uniform: the low-hanging jeans, runners, and baseball cap that symbolize group solidarity. He then gives me his phone number and tells me to call him after I have made the purchase.

How fast can you make a beeline to the nearest department store? It depends on where you live, but I'm there in a resounding twenty minutes. I look first for the jeans and try on a pair. I have a 28-inch waist, so I try on a 32. Man, these are loose, but after I put a belt through them, they hang about an inch below my boxer shorts. Perfect! Then I try on runners and find the black baseball cap to top off the outfit. Total cost is just under $100. I phone Shane.

"Meet us at the corner of Davie and Denman tomorrow at four p.m. sharp. Mark often takes a walk through Stanley Park on Mondays, and that is where the fight will happen," Shane explains.

"I can't make four p.m.; that's when I'm in aikido."

"Freedom, get your priorities straight. You can miss a class of aikido for this. Be there and wear your new uniform." *Click*.

Okay, the message is undeniably clear. My heart sinks as I contemplate the shifting priorities of life. Nonetheless, I am going through with this. When I wake in the morning, I put on my new jeans, runners, cap, and an old tank-top undershirt, and head downstairs for breakfast. Star opens her mouth, but before she can utter a word, I tell her, "Shut *up!*"

"That is no way to talk to your sister—apologize right now," Mom commands.

"No way. She's an egghead and I don't want to hear her beak off."

"I wasn't planning to 'beak off.' I just wanted to say I like your new look. What's up with it?" Star responds.

"None of your business. I simply wanted a change. Anything wrong with that?"

Neither Mom nor Star say anything. Instead, I notice them both recoil slightly, looking stunned at my reaction. I'm not having a reaction…I just want to be left alone right now. I have a lot on my mind.

It's 3:30 p.m., the bell rings, and school is out for the day. I feel excited and scared. As soon as I'm outside, I pull off my tank top and feel my hard-packed abs as I begin heading toward the rendezvous point. Wearing these clothes with my shirt off helps me overcome the fear as I catch others checking out my new look. Wow, I've never been eyed like this before! A few babes whistle at me as they drive by, and I have to say I like the attention. I never strutted down so many streets before either. When I arrive, Shane and Cory are there to greet me. Mike apparently got into some kind of trouble last night and he wouldn't be joining us.

Before I could ask about this, we begin walking into Stanley Park, and Shane kicks in with, "Okay, this is how it's going to look. We will be hiding behind some bushes, and when we see Mark walk by, you step out in front of him and make eye contact. He will know what it's about as soon as he sees your uniform. Mark beat up Mike real bad a few months ago, and he would be stupid to think we would not eventually get revenge. The fight continues until either one of you gives up or is unconscious. Got it?"

"…Yeah, I get it."

I hope this will be over quickly. In some ways, I can't believe I'm involved in this, and I just want it done. I will soon have my wish, as they see Mark a short distance away and tap me on the shoulder to point him out to me. Well, I know what I have to do. As soon as he is a few yards away, I push through the brush and plant my feet in front of him, staring in his eyes as I do so. Shocked at first, he recomposes himself and strips to the waist, exposing his massive chest and bulging biceps.

In keeping with my training, I actually wait for him to make the first move. As he throws his first punch, I circle to the side, grab his arm, and twist it enough to make him flip over. I allow him to get back on his feet as I prepare for his next attack. I see his adrenalin intensify as his anger mounts and he bursts into a stance that tells me he's planning to deliver a series of blows to my midsection. As he makes the lunge, I again step out of the way of his fists and create a right-arm lock while simultaneously tripping him. I then put all of my attention to bending back his wrist until he pleads for surrender.

At that moment, Shane and Cory come out from the brush and together decide that Mark needs more punishment. After delivering several hard kicks and punches, they motion for me to escape, and the three of us run out of there fast.

It's been a long time since I felt my own adrenalin rush so intensely! We end up at Sunset Beach, lungs heaving, sweating profusely, and breaking into fits of crazy laughter and crude humour. Shane compliments me on a job well done, although he tells me I should have hurt him more. I don't respond to that, and in fact I would prefer not to think about the fighting at all. Relieved that it's over would be more accurate.

"You have finished the first and hardest part of your initiation, Freedom."

"First part, Shane? What else must I do?" I ask, ashamedly.

He pulls out a pack of Export As. He gives one to Cory and takes one for himself. Then he asks, "Ever smoke before, Freedom?"

"No, I haven't."

"I didn't think so." He then pulls out another cigarette and offers it to me. "Make sure you inhale."

I take it, and he lights my cigarette first before Cory's and his own.

Shit, I never wanted to smoke, and I can't believe I am about to without giving it any forethought. I also know this is not the time to chicken out. I inhale.

I feel nauseated and lightheaded, and my skin colour turns green. I nearly vomit. Maybe I'll pass out. I don't, but wish I could. Coughing, and more coughing. I want to stop. Shane tells me to keep smoking till it's done. My head is swimming, my pulse is up, and I'm feeling wobbly. I don't ever want another cigarette in my life. They laugh as they see me struggle with this one cig.

"You'll get used to it," Cory reassures me. "It only took me a few until I adjusted. Don't worry—you're with us."

"Yeah, Freedom. You passed your initiation. You're now a member of our gang. *Yip yip yap yappity yap!*" Shane bellows. "Welcome, comrade!"

I try to shake off the strange sensations in my head and body while I begin appreciating that I did it! I'm now a member of one of the coolest gangs in the city. This is going to be more fun than I expected—at least that is what I would like to believe. Reality and fantasy, of course, are not always the same. Time may tell a different story, but for right now, I embellish a feeling I've never had before. This is *my* gang, and these are *my* people.

"Freedom, we are going to be spending a lot of time together," Shane begins. "Two things: First, every day at lunch time, you are to work out in your school's weight room. You already have a good physique, but you're going to need more muscle. Second, every day when you're done school, you meet up with us at four. We hang out together Monday to Friday until six." He sees the aghast look on my face and adds, "I know you have been into aikido, but now it is time for us to teach you some real fighting. Think of this as the next level in your training."

I nod my head, but only half-heartedly. I'm not sure I've made the right decision, but at least I've made one. Many decisions in life are made like that really.

Before heading for home, I tell Shane, "Listen, I'll be late on Wednesday. I need to make an appearance at the dojo and tell Sensei that I'll be moving on. Okay?"

"Yeah, no problem," Shane replies. "Meet us at five instead, at the corner of Thurlow and Pacific. Our clubhouse is near there."

The next two days I obsess about how I am going to tell Sensei that I quit. Aikido has meant everything to me for nearly a year, but I must now move on. Such anguishing doesn't help because Wednesday comes anyway.

I leave school a bit early so that I can arrive at the dojo before everyone else gets there. Sensei is sitting at his desk, and as soon as he sees me, he motions for me to come over.

As I start to—

"*Stop!* Shoes, Freedom!"

I can't believe I forgot. I guess I've had too much on my mind.

"Why you dress like that?" Sensei asks. "You look like punk."

"I was ready for a change, and that is why I came early today. I need to talk to you," I say sheepishly.

"*No!* My answer *no*, Freedom. This is not time. You too close to black to end here."

"I'm sorry, but I need to end it here, Sensei."

"Why? What in your head? Um, maybe you found 'babe'—that what you call woman, Freedom?"

"Uh, yeah, that's right." I now wish my baseball cap would hide my face altogether. "But no, that is not the reason. I'm leaving aikido because I need to grow in a different direction for a while. I have made other commitments, and I must now oblige them."

"You not understand commitment, Freedom. Here… right here…this commitment. You and me and discipline of aikido."

I feel my eyes water as I stand my ground with Sensei. "I must move on…period."

My eyes are like sand compared to Sensei's. I never saw him cry before, and as they stream down his cheeks, he reaches over to embrace me. The only thing stronger than my self-doubt right now is my need to belong to a peer group. I welcome his embrace, and for a few moments, I don't want this to ever end. However, goodbye is goodbye, and I pull myself together enough to leave when I notice the others arriving.

I try not to be spotted by any of them, but I think Chris sees me. From the corner of my eye, I feel his deep gaze at my new uniform, perhaps one he recognizes from the west end neighbourhood. I hope that does not create repercussions for me.

I meet up with the gang at 5 p.m., and Shane immediately offers me a cigarette. I reluctantly take it from him, light it, and again work at smoking and inhaling. It's a little easier than yesterday, but I still don't see the point of creating such a foul taste in my mouth. Nonetheless, I guess it's part of what the gang does, and what the gang does, I do.

We head over to the clubhouse, which is actually a large shed in Mike's backyard. Aside from some lawn paraphernalia, most of the shed is empty, except for four folding chairs that we sit on. Cigarette butts litter the floor, and I soon learn that smoking and drinking beer are two of the gang's favourite pastimes. I find out that the three of them are each sixteen, but Shane looks older and he bootlegs for the rest of us. When we're not smoking and drinking, we're usually on the prowl for babes first and fighting second. It doesn't take long until I am confronted with two things that seem completely out of sync with one another: conflict with the law and the prospect of losing my virginity.

First the good news. Her name is Ventura, and she is

originally from Puerto Rico. She attends my school in ninth grade and I find out she has been checking me out ever since I started using the weight room several weeks ago. She also knows I belong to the gang. Well, no time for details here, but let me just say that she moans even louder than I do! Like a burning candle, however, the flame of raw passion seems to flicker far too early and she moves on after knowing me for a week—but what a week!

Now the bad news. Sometimes we do things in gangs we would never think of doing alone. Fighting is a good example of this. I have been learning to fight better, but mostly street style. Cory always said that experience is the best teacher, and although I am not sure I believe him entirely, I am winning more fights than I am losing. The trouble is, trouble is trouble, and sometimes things get a little carried away. Just like at home.

I shouldn't have been that surprised when the police arrived at our doorstep.

Just my luck, Dad answers the door. He is shocked to see the cops standing there. He blurts out, "*I didn't do anything!*"

They look at him like he's lost his mind. My opinion is that he has. What the police don't know is that he just smoked a huge doobie and the roach is still sitting in the kitchen. Perhaps Dad is just a little paranoid. Ha ha, serves him right.

"We're looking for Freedom Bates. Does he live here?"

"Yes. *Freedom, come here!*" Dad bumps into me as I anxiously step forward. "Oh, you're right there."

The taller officer speaks, "Freedom Bates, you are being

charged with assault causing bodily harm. You have the right to remain silent. Anything you say can and will be used against you in a court of law. You have the right to speak to an attorney, and to have an attorney present during any questioning. If you cannot afford a lawyer, one will be provided for you at government expense...."

Dad looks at me with piercing bloodshot eyes, looking shocked beyond description. I simply reach for a shirt, put on my flip-flops, and go peacefully with the two officers. After spending a few hours at the station, I'm released on my own recognizance. What I faced there was nothing like the interrogation I received at home from Mom and Dad.

"Tell us exactly what you did, Freedom," Mom demands of me.

"I kicked some guy in the head a few times after he tried to stab me—that's all."

After telling them the whole story, Dad screams, *"Freedom, you are to quit this gang immediately!"*

"You can both go to hell! I will do what I damn well please!" I scream back. My blood is really boiling. "Remember your own words: 'We will provide you helpful suggestions regarding your decisions, Freedom, but it is always your choice what you ultimately decide to do.'"

That works, as Mom and Dad both storm from the room. I know this is not the end of it.

Actually, the next four years was like this between my parents and me as I continued my allegiance to the gang. By the time I turned eighteen, I had already spent several weeks cumulatively in child detention centres and watched

Shane, Mike, and Cory periodically spend time in adult jail.

It shouldn't surprise you to hear that Mom and Dad have decided to move back to the U.S., to somewhere in Connecticut where Dad was raised. They will be gone in three weeks, and I can't wait. They have been nothing but a thorn in my side for such a long time.

Chapter 4

ENDINGS

Do you know what the view is like from behind bars? It ain't pretty. I'm nineteen now and I've been serving a three-month sentence for assault. There's no point going into all of the details that landed me here, but I'll tell you this much: this is no place to get rehabilitated. I was only in for a few hours before landing in my first fight. Two guys jumped me, thinking I looked like someone who would sit back and be their "boy." I am nobody's boy, I'll tell you that. I took them both down hard and fast, and since then, other inmates have left me alone. Like I said earlier, sometimes life is about winning or losing, and I'm not about to lose.

You probably wouldn't be surprised to hear that cigarettes are easy to get here. In fact, they sell them at the canteen cheaper than at most convenience stores! It's funny how the habit creeps up on you. I used to only smoke when I was with the gang, but now I smoke a pack a day with or without them, and sometimes more when I'm stressed. I'm not stressed right now, but I am wanting out of here. What a waste of time!

While incarcerated, I hear that Dad is gravely ill. His

physician told him he may only have a few months to live.

"Your father has lung cancer. The doctor said smoking both cigarettes and pot caused it," Mom tells me on the phone.

"I really don't care, Mom," I blurt out. "Dad hurt us more than enough with his drug use to last a lifetime."

"Freedom, besides his trouble keeping steady employment, how did he ever hurt you?"

"He wasn't there for me when I most needed him, Mom. I can't count the times he was too wrecked to talk intelligibly when I needed his opinion on something. It seemed both of you would rather smoke than make time for either me or Star during our early years," I stated matter-of-factly.

"Freedom, he has asked that you come to visit him. He needs to say goodbye to you."

Choked, I gasp for enough air to say, "It's too late for that, Mom. Dad said goodbye to me a long time ago." *Click.* Hanging up on the phone on your Mom is one of the hardest things I ever learned to do. At least plenty of practice has made it easier over the years.

I get out of prison on August 31, 1985, and the fresh air of freedom is almost more than I can take. In fact, I cough a lot more than I used to—something about doing time made me smoke more, and I only hope that I can get back to a pack a day.

At least the summer isn't over. I decide to take the next few weeks to simply work on a tan and live off the little cash I have in the bank. I'm trying to get my life together, and I know that one thing I must do is leave the gang. I phone Shane and he answers on the first ring.

"Hey, Freedom, nice to hear from you! So glad you're back on the street. Cory is finally out too, so I think it's time for a little celebration. Meet at my place nine-ish."

"Sorry, Shane. I had time to do a lot of thinking, and I need to move on. Sayonara." *Click.*

This is not the time to entertain idle whining about "why now?" "reconsider this," "have you thought of that?" or simply "don't leave." The one thing I can feel good about is that I have always been decisive, and once my mind is made up, there is no turning back. No turning back. When my mind is made up about something important, there is no turning back.

I don't answer any of Shane's incessant attempts to reach me. Finally, I am fed up enough to block future calls from his number, and those of Mike and Cory as well. I'm done; I'm so done with them. Having a criminal record is not going to make finding a job any easier after I enjoy some summer fun.

The next month is about cruising for babes and getting laid as much as a nineteen-year-old should. I turn twenty really soon, and something about the transition to no longer being a teenager is having an effect on me. I suspect I will have to start getting my act together.

Three in the morning is never a good time to awaken, especially not to the sound of a hysterical mother. I will re-member September 19 for a long time.

"Dad died an hour ago. I gave him some water, and as he lay down, his spirit sang its last song…. Freedom, are you still there…? Are you still there, Freedom?"

I can't answer, my mouth frozen for a moment in time.

My whimper was all my mom could hear, and it's all I could say. As though I'd had too many cold frothy beers throughout a blizzard's night, I quietly hang up the phone after mumbling the word "la-terrr."

I feel nauseated and lightheaded, and my skin colour turns green. I nearly vomit. Maybe I'll pass out. I don't, but wish I could. Coughing, more coughing. I want to stop. My head is swimming, my pulse is up, and I'm feeling wobbly. No one is laughing this time.

I light up a cigarette and inhale it more deeply than ever. I don't feel anything, really, like falling into a vortex of spinning debris. There is no end and no beginning, just the realization that what is *is*, and what is not *is not*. I need to shake this, and I know exactly how to do it. It's called denial, and it's the perfect way to self-deceive and create perpetual half-truths.

Chapter 5
THE MELTDOWN

Smoking seems like the least of my worries, and I have no intention of quitting. For the next two years, I spend most nights at the local pub two blocks from where I live. It's pretty scuzzy, but you get used to it. The stupid tables are covered with absorbent felt so that when bums like me spill their beer, it doesn't really matter. Feeling sorry for myself again, I truly wonder what does…matter.

Little purpose or meaning is found at the bottom of another empty glass. After many such glasses, I sure feel aggressive. Wow, all the testosterone rages through my drunken stupor, but I can still deliver one of the best punches and kicks around this neck of the woods. Take me on, I dare you, but know that you might be missing more than just a few teeth by the time I'm finished with ya. Yeah, I don't just talk big—I've learned to become a force to be reckoned with.

Nights don't scare me, but one night the chill inside is sharper than the outside air when I hear, "Freedom, is that you? God, it is you! I haven't seen you in years. Where have you been?"

I nearly crap myself I am so shocked to hear someone call me by name. I turn around and see Chris standing there. Staggering to embrace him, I nearly fall before we connect.

"Can I walk you home? Wouldn't be the first time, eh?" he asks, chuckling.

"That would be nice, Chris. Great running into you. I'm between jobs right now and just felt like celebrating tonight before I get serious. What's new with you?"

"I'm in my third year of engineering at the University of British Columbia. One more year and I'll be done," he boasts unintentionally.

"Wow, that's great, Chris. Good going! Anyway, this is my place, so maybe I'll see you again sometime."

"Great running into you, Freedom. Sensei often asked about you while I was still taking classes at the dojo, but I had nothing to tell him. I know you got involved in that gang—hey, are you still involved with them?"

"No, I left the gang two years ago. Anyway, Chris, gotta go!" I couldn't wait to get away from him, actually. Hearing about his success left me with a sunken feeling, one I wanted to shake as quickly as possible. For me, it's just another Tuesday night. For Chris, it's another day forward toward graduating with something substantial.

The next day, I wake up determined to get my life together. After a few cigarettes and my morning beer, I get dressed and begin looking for work. A nearby Starbucks is looking for someone to work noon till 8 p.m., and I figure these are exactly the hours I need right now.

After my shift, I head to the pub to ease the stress I feel inside. I actually do feel much calmer after six pints and half a pack of Export As. Buddy at the next table gets up to head to the bar and nearly falls into my lap as he staggers to get past me.

"*Get the fuck off me, you stupid ass!*" I yell. The entire bar turns around to see what the commotion is all about.

"Ah, sorry, dude. Need ta watch where I'm going. Headin' for another beer—you want one?"

"Yeah, thanks. I'm drinking Bud," I say.

After that beer, I leave realizing that I've probably had a couple too many. Again, I feel the chill once I get outside. I look around, but there is no one there this time. I go home and pass out.

Work is actually not going well. Customers are really pissing me off, and my blood is beginning to boil. They think they can tell me I'm too slow, their coffee is too hot, their coffee is not hot enough, it tastes like it has been sitting too long, or whatever—enough! I didn't take this job to take a bunch of crap from anyone. I'm trying to hold back, but it's all I can do to keep my mouth shut and get out of there to relieve some stress at the watering hole.

I am so tensed up that I end up taking my frustration out on other bar patrons. A few more drinks and I feel myself seething inside. Even I know I had best be going home soon. I mean if you aren't in control of yourself, who is?

While contemplating whether I should have one more drink before I call it a night, a guy has the audacity to spill his drink on me as he pushes by to meet up with his friends. Instinctively, I get up and shove him several feet until he is up against the wall. My red eyes glare at him, my look hardly a match for his own. The bar owner sees where this is headed and yells, "Take it outside and don't come back here tonight—neither one of you!"

We exit to the back alley, each hell-bent on hurting the other. He pulls out a switchblade, darting it to and fro, threatening me and preparing to lunge. I stare at his "centre," a place approximately two inches below the navel. From here, I can anticipate his move nearly as soon as he initiates it. His thrust is intended to connect to my stomach, and I quickly pivot to the left and allow his momentum to carry through so that he falls hard in front of me on the pavement. Now that he's down, I begin releasing my rage on him, and when I am done, he's not moving.

A moment of rationality rattles my inebriated psyche, and I get down on my knees to check his pulse. Thank God he's still breathing! I notice a small butterfly tattoo above his wrist, thinking that it seems a bit odd for someone so rugged. Anyway, I know I need to get out of there quickly, so I leave and make an anonymous 911 call when I get home. I don't know the outcome, and would rather not know. What I do know is that I need to find a different watering hole.

The agitation in my life isn't getting better. Anger is often the first thing I wake up to and the last thing I fall to sleep with. I don't remember ever feeling this way before. Drinking feels like both the solution and the problem. It helps take the edge off the deep sense of inner turmoil I feel, but it also allows anger to surface more readily. I find a different pub to call home, only a block from the one I used to frequent. When I leave there, I continue to feel the chill of someone's presence, lingering sometimes until I get home. Another manifestation of inner turmoil, I conclude. "Why am I feeling so unsettled these days, and where is all this anger coming from?" I ask myself repeatedly. No answers come, so I simply do my best to cope with what I'm experiencing.

Being stuck is when every day and every night looks exactly the same. Eventually, however, what goes around comes around. That happens on March 28, 1987. I'm liquored up more than usual, and as I leave the pub, three guys follow me outside. As I turn around to face them, the heavier-set guy speaks.

"You don't remember us, do you?" he beaks off. "We're Rex's friends, the guy you beat up a few months ago. Rex still has flashbacks of the night you sent him to the hospital. Now it's time for justice…eh, boys?" The other two acknowledge the come on.

I am so stunned by what I hear that the momentary lapse in my centre is enough for the three of them to get in one blow after another. As I begin to lose consciousness, I have the slightest awareness of someone joining us.

Ever have the experience of thinking you are dreaming something that is actually really happening to you? My dream has Sensei in it, and he is saying to me, "Breathe, Freedom! Breathe! Let smoke clear out of your life. See again…breathe again. Breathe now…please."

My eyes begin opening to the blurry image of Sensei holding my head. "Sen…sei, is…that…you?"

"Yes, Freedom, it is. I follow you for months. Dark spirits have risen within you. Chris phoned me and spoke of this shadow that haunts you."

"I…need…help, Sen…sei. I'm…out of…control."

"Don't speak, Freedom. Just breathe. Talk later. No time for talk now."

My next memory is awakening in a hospital bed. A gorgeous nurse stands over me, staring at my bare chest, which looks as black and blue as I feel inside. The first thought that enters my mind is being a child naked on Wreck Beach with my parents, and as my dad's face comes into better focus, I begin weeping as I lie there. The nurse assumes I am in too much physical pain, and as she adds more Demerol to my intravenous drip, I begin feeling light-headed and surreal. The next few hours roll into one as I lose all perspective of time and space.

The next day is much better, as my consciousness returns to normal. Dr. Michaels, my family physician, enters the room along with two other men dressed in white lab coats.

"Freedom, thankfully your injuries are not life threatening," Dr. Michaels says. "You have suffered a mild concussion and you have two bruised ribs. The bruising is quite deep around your chest and stomach, but it's nothing to worry about. We are concerned about some of your internal organs, however, and consequently, we will be running further tests over the next few days as we keep a close watch on you. If you feel strong enough to get out of bed and walk, do so, but stay within the confines of this nursing unit."

"What kind of damage, Doctor?" I ask with trepidation in my voice.

"The urinalysis tells us that your kidneys are not working properly. This could be temporary from the blows you sustained, but we aren't sure yet. Furthermore, your lungs appear darkened in the x-rays, and we are concerned about a couple of spots. Are you a smoker, Freedom?"

"Yes, Dr. Michaels, I am. I began smoking when I was thirteen."

"Have you thought about quitting?"

"No I haven't and I don't intend to either. Given my lifestyle, smoking is the least of my worries. Heck, I almost just got killed in a back-alley fight! I have more important things to think about right now."

Dr. Michaels backs off and soon leaves my room. For a few moments, I think about the many ways we get people to leave us alone when we don't want to face up to something. I soon move on to thinking about other things. Especially bothersome are intrusive thoughts about my dad. Why is this happening? He was such a loser, yet I feel my eyes about to explode again with another shower. The floodgates open and I cry silently in a bed that suddenly feels too small. I get up, feeling pain surge through my torso. The mirror doesn't show how beat up I really feel right now: it doesn't show the inside of my emotions.

I notice the housecoat and the ugly slippers (if they even deserve to be called that) the nurse has left for me. Screw it—I traipse into the hallway wearing only the hospital bottoms. I notice that I'm being checked out by several nurses, but no one says anything. Knowing that they think I'm hot is actually helping me feel better inside! If nothing else, it's a great distraction.

Behind me I hear the familiar sound of footsteps, lifting my spirits as the presence of a great person does to everyone of us. I turn around beaming as I grimace in pain to welcome my Sensei.

"Surprised to see you out of bed this soon, Freedom. This is good, yes?"

"Yes it is, Sensei. However, they will be running more tests on me over the next few days. Everything is okay though."

"How you know?" His words squeeze between pursed lips.

"Of course. I know my body and it tells me everything is fine. I just need to recover from my wounds."

"How deep are your wounds, Freedom?"

I can't speak for a few moments as his words rupture my composure. I manage to shake it off, but only manage to utter with a strange sense of surrender. "I don't know."

"When you leave here, you come back to dojo. It time for you to reconnect with your destiny."

"I must return to bed; I'm feeling faint." Before I can collapse, Sensei puts his arm around my shoulder, giving me the extra strength I need while I shake off the wobbly feeling that soon begins to pass. I lie in bed while Sensei continues to talk to me, showing me the compassion that he taught me several years ago.

Before he leaves, he says, "I see you soon, Freedom— at dojo." He bows, and I nod my head as though I were doing the same.

The next day, they wheel me off for some kind of scan. They lay me flat and tell me not to move. The machine looks rather intimidating, like I'm about to enter a huge doughnut. Once I'm in place, I am told to shut my eyes and keep them closed until the scan is complete. The technologist tells me my doctor will have the results later today.

As I get wheeled back to my room, I am both shocked and delighted to see Star waiting for me. "Mom was unable to come," she begins, "but she asked me to pass on her love and her concern for you. It is so nice to see you again, Freedom."

I swear I should be locked up in the psychiatric ward. Star has the intuition to know she should embrace me, and as she does, I cry until her shoulder is completely soaked. I finally get my choked up words out. "Thank you for coming, Star. I've missed you so much."

"Mom and I have missed you more than you can imagine, Freedom. Frankly, Mom is still a mess following Dad's death and that's the real reason she couldn't accompany me."

"I understand. I'll phone her soon; I just have a few of my own issues to resolve first."

Our visit continues for the next hour and a half, and although we catch up on each other's lives, we carefully avoid confronting the anger that we both feel: her toward me for not coming to visit after Dad's diagnosis and after his death, and me toward Dad for reasons I do not fully understand.

After Star leaves, I get out of bed again to walk down to the patient lounge to watch some television. Mindless images flash across the screen while I remain in a rather stunned shallow state, hardly noticing a world beyond myself. I am thrown back into reality when I hear a nurse's voice on the intercom: "Freedom, Dr. Michaels is here to see you. Please return to your room."

Chapter 6

HEALING THROUGH FIGHTING

I sit on the edge of my bed while Dr. Michaels begins. "I now have the results from your scan and the urinalysis you had earlier. Your kidneys are functioning normally again, so that is a relief. Your lungs, however, are black from excessive smoking. The spots we found are actually tar deposits. There are no signs of cancer at this time, and if you quit smoking, your lungs will clean out most of this debris."

"Does that mean I can check out of the hospital now?" I ask calmly.

"Yes, I will discharge you."

"Thank you, Dr. Michaels. I'm very relieved."

While the discharge papers are being prepared, I get dressed in my street clothes and wait in the patient lounge. After a half hour or so, I hear on the intercom: "Freedom, please come to the nursing station for discharge." The attendant gives me a pamphlet about quitting smoking. I thank her, and I place it in my back pocket. Once outside, I strip off my shirt, light up a cigarette, and begin the long walk home. My chest still hurts because of the bruised ribs, so I walk a little slower than usual.

I hear someone running behind me yelling out, "Freedom! Freedom! Wait up!"

There really are times you wish you didn't have to run into certain people. Why does Chris always need to be there when I'm in a moment of weakness? God, I hate that! It's bad enough that I have shown weakness in front of Sensei, but does the whole world need to know everything about me? Well, that's how it feels sometimes, even though I know it isn't true.

"Hi, Chris. Nice running into you," I lie.

"Always my pleasure. Hey, what happened to your chest? Have you been beat up or what?"

I really hate questions like that. Perhaps if I could think quickly enough on my feet, I could come up with a good comeback line. Well I can't, so I tell him the truth: "Yes, I was beat up and just got out of the hospital. I'm okay now, and as soon as I recover fully, I'm planning to return to aikido."

"Wow, I'm really sorry to hear about the beating, and I'm glad you're okay. I think the idea of returning to aikido is awesome, and funny you mention this. I've been thinking about getting back to it myself. Would it be okay if we return to Hiro's studio together? Having you accompany me will really help my motivation."

"Sure, Chris," I reply. "That sounds like a great idea. I have always valued our connection. What's your phone number? I'll call you as soon as my ribs heal." I write his number down and provide him mine as well. We say goodbye, and I continue walking home.

In retrospect, I'm glad I ran into Chris. He has always

been a true friend, despite the fact that we have never spent time together outside of the dojo. I think I should change that now.

Star will be staying with me for the next few days, and she is a great help to me while I continue recovering. We share a great deal about our lives with each other and have come to a deeper place of mutual respect. She is making a name for herself as a hair stylist; her clientele includes several local celebrities. She hopes that she will make a still bigger name for herself over time.

I feel I have so much less to be proud of, as most of my hopes and dreams are future oriented. I still don't know what I want to be when I grow up, and at twenty-one, I feel really behind in life. Star reminds me that there are times when you need to focus on healing and that this is one of those times for me. I guess she's right sometimes. (I hate to admit that—remember, she *is* still my sister!)

Anyway, I'm very sad now that she has to leave. At the airport, we both soak each other's shoulder while we say goodbye. A deep ache still lurks inside me. I know so much of it has to do with conflicting feelings I still harbour toward Dad.

After another week, I'm ready to get back to aikido. I first phone Chris and confirm that he is indeed interested in coming with me. Then I call Sensei to find out when we may begin.

"I very, very happy to hear both you come back. Come to dojo tomorrow seven p.m. for adult class," he says heartily.

"Thank you, Sensei. See you then." *Click.*

Neither Chris nor I have a *gi* that fits, so we each take jogging pants and skintight tank tops with us to wear in class. This is a beginner aikido class for adults, and although the routine isn't difficult, I find myself constantly out of breath and even wheezing at times. My panting sounds nearly desperate, and I wonder if I will finish the class at this rate, not to mention that I'm also craving a cigarette. I know I'm a little out of shape, but I also know my stamina will return with regular training.

At the end of class, Sensei asks for both of us to see him. He says, "Welcome back to dojo. You ready for purchase *gi*?"

We both nod our heads, and Sensei goes to his back room to bring us our new uniforms. After buying them, we stand and bow, preparing to exit.

"Freedom, stay. More for us to talk about," Sensei says.

As I watch Chris leave, I feel apprehensive, wondering what Sensei wants of me. I watch Sensei's bottom lip curl, but the look on his face tells me I am about to receive a major lesson. I want to turn around and run, but I remain respectful toward the man who saved my life.

He begins, "I hear many stories about you, Freedom— none good. Are these the lies of bad gossip?"

"No, Sensei, I suspect you have heard correctly."

"How does inflicting pain onto another man help heal your own?"

Dazed by his question, I answer, "I don't know what you mean, Sensei."

"Who is bully now, Freedom?"

Pausing, I respond, "I am. I have become the bully."

"Exactly. That which you suffered now you make others suffer. Time to learn basics of compassion."

"What?" I say, becoming more confused.

"Freedom, your father died recently. Is this correct?"

"He died nearly two years ago, and good riddance."

"Your father did like most did not. Most simply threw out the sixties—including the good. Things like protesting wrongdoings of others, standing strong in commitment for peace, loving others in many ways. Unfortunately, he also hurt himself from that culture, the marijuana and the smoking."

"Dad was also a lousy breadwinner, Sensei. We nearly couldn't pay our bills every month."

"Did you feel hungry, Freedom?"

"No."

"Did you feel father did not love you?"

"No, I never felt that way actually."

"Then you must overcome bad feelings toward father."

"What do you mean, Sensei?"

"What is your problem with father? He against violence in any form, then you betray teaching and become violent. Is this right way to honour father? Many years ago, I say respect your father. It too bad you not understand this lesson. Your father loved you with whole heart, yet you disrespect him for pot use and trouble with jobs. Forces of good and evil always fight in mortal combat. Your father not perfect, and I hope mirror show you same now."

Like a karate chop breaking through many pieces of wood, Sensei shatters many layers of denial with his single comment, and I feel more naked standing there than I ever felt on Wreck Beach during my growing years. As his words penetrate my thick skull, I feel a psychosomatic collapse begin as I fall to my knees and begin crying uncontrollably.

After a few minutes of gut-wrenching sobbing, Sensei asserts: "*Stop, Freedom*, and breathe. Let the smoke inside clear. Breathe, Freedom. *Breathe Freedom and stop!* It time to stop crying and regain composure. Lesson only beginning."

My ears are open and my heart is broken by his words of wisdom, and I bow my head, too ashamed to show him the tears that keep running down my cheeks.

Sensei continues, "Listen to me, Freedom: Only real enemy is one inside, and it teach you this through your recklessness—the smoking, the drinking, the fighting. You have fought false enemy. Time to redirect, refocus, and realize only true enemy.

"Your actions give voice to innermost mind and feelings. If you sow seeds of aggression, that is what you will get back. If you sow seeds of love, that you get back too. Which seed you plant now? Your life reflect what seed you sow.

"A teacher appear when ready for next lesson. When ready, you cannot avoid teacher from appearing. It is cause and effect," Sensei explains. "To heal and grow in aikido, you need stop smoking. Your breathing too laboured in today's class."

"It would be easier to stop drinking, Sensei," I reply. "Although I have certainly abused alcohol, I never became addicted to it. However, most smokers *are* addicted to nicotine, and I am one of them."

"It time you learn to live up to your name. You not free from guilt, not free of negative mind, not free from cigarettes. I know someone who help you quit, and I help too."

"Sensei, how would you know anything about quitting? I respect you immensely for your knowledge of aikido, but smoking?"

"This is much of your problem, Freedom. You only know me as Sensei. You not know the other wisdoms I have. Like your concept of *enemy*. Where is *this* enemy, Freedom? You been deceived. People you think are enemy are people like you. They people with many good qualities, but you only focus on qualities you do not like. From this, you create fiction you call 'enemy.' The enemies only live in your mind. There is *true* enemy in your life, however. It called smoking.

"Till now, your aikido has been self-defense and self-control, but now time you learn how to *really* conquer enemy, the enemy that is *not* a person. Freedom, time you learn to beat crap out of cigarettes. You ready for *real* combat?"

"It's not that simple, Sensei. I have many good reasons why I smoke. Maybe I need to be a rebel, and smoking allows me to be that."

"Freedom, you be rebel and be non-smoker. Many constructive ways to channel the part of you that does not want to 'fit in.' Gandhi was rebel, and look at his accomplishment. Many great world leaders were great rebels, yet they made difference because their rebelliousness was not from self-hate but instead from enlightened self-love."

With my attention still riveted on every word after so many absent years, I hear Sensei yet I am not ready to cave. I continue, "Smoking helps me cope with stress, and lately I've been experiencing a lot of it."

"Don't believe nonsense, Freedom. I know those who not smoke have less stress. What you think is *stress relief* is *addiction relief*—cigarette reduce craving—that is all," Sensei explains.

"Well, cigarettes help me socialize," I say, scrambling to come up with some good reason for continuing to smoke, "and they improve my concentration."

"How does smoking make knowing people easier or better, Freedom? Most public places stop your smoke now, and the smoker is judged badly. Is smoking becoming more acceptable or less?"

"Less."

"Exactly. You also mention concentrate, so concentrate for this moment in time. No study shown smokers concentrate better than non-smokers. Might there be better reason you think it help you concentrate, Freedom?"

"Hmm, maybe because a cigarette takes the edge off the withdrawal that keeps returning after smoking the previous cigarette?"

"Very good, Freedom—now you use big head. You ever think smoke help you become more alert, it only very, very big addiction you experiencing."

"Smoking helps me kill time. It also helps me deal with my boredom."

"Yes, but smoking also kill host too. Average smoker who get disease die fourteen years less than what God give.

Quality of life not good if you can't breathe good. More time when you quit smoking, Freedom—time to enjoy life and do thing with meaning, purpose."

"Okay, I can buy all of that. But I don't want to gain fat if I quit smoking and everyone I know who has quit has put on weight."

"Good try, Freedom. Most people do gain few pounds after quit. Body slow down, like your brain past few years, slow down and appetite little more. All masters agree: best to quit smoking then lose weight later. Remember, Freedom, stopping smoking *most* important thing do to improve health. Smoking worst cause of disease in world! Priority one is quit first, then do other goals after."

"Is there nothing I can do to keep my hard-packed abs while I quit, Sensei?"

"There is. Some medication help. My friend can tell you everything you need know. No more excuses. Now is time to quit, yes?"

The one thing about Sensei is that he doesn't let you get away with bullshit, which is unlike most people I know. Nonetheless, I'm not going to let Sensei win this battle.

"You don't understand, Sensei. I enjoy smoking. I like it, and I don't want to quit!"

"Tell me, Freedom. Did you enjoy first cigarette?"

"Hmm, no. I thought I was going to be sick."

"Exactly. Do you think cigarette was trying to tell you something first time?"

"Well, it was certainly making me aware that the smoke was poisoning my body."

"Okay, you enjoy *every* cigarette you smoke? You ever

smoke just to feed addiction or habit?"

"Yeah, I have to admit that. I suspect half the time, I'm smoking just to avoid nicotine withdrawal and taper the urge that builds inside me."

"What name for urge to smoke, Freedom?"

"We call it addiction, Sensei."

"Exactly. When decide to quit, you must decide to never smoke again. Do not take lightly. Do not take this lightly, Freedom. Addiction more serious than habit, and when addicted to something, must make decision to quit entirely. Some successfully reduce smoking amount, but most not succeed. Even those who do, they continue to have more diseases because of smoke. *Only* decision is quit permanently—no puff, no cheat, no smoke, period."

"Okay, maybe I'll just quit on my own. I don't need help to do this."

"Not true, Freedom. Fact: fewer than ten percent of people who quit smoking alone, with no help from anyone, still not smoke year later. Listen to me: my friend and me, we help you fight and win this one."

"Anything else, Sensei?" I say impatiently as I tire of hearing about this.

"Yes, there is," Sensei adds. "Besides excuses for thinking you should smoke, might there be deep meaning and purpose in quitting?"

"No, I don't think so."

"Think about it. What your father die from?"

"Lung cancer."

"What caused it?"

"You know what caused it, Sensei."

"Yes. Do you know others who died or became sick because of smoke, Freedom?"

"Yes, I imagine most people do."

"Perhaps quitting smoke a tribute to others you know who died or who are sick. Perhaps it deeper than that, Freedom. Maybe it becomes greater tribute to your well-being, your self-respect, and your self-love to stop. Perhaps you take step now because you learn what loving means. Now is time for freedom. Why be addict to drug that does not even get you high?"

"You sound a bit like Dad with that last comment, Sensei," I say somewhat humorously.

"It true though, correct? Smoking hurt pocketbook and health, right now and future. What it give you back that positive, healthy, or worth salvaging?"

"You've got me on that one. I feel like such a failure actually, in so many areas of my life. Smoking reminds me of this every time I light one up."

"Therefore, you have nothing to lose. After you quit, you accomplish important goal. Then appreciate success."

"You're right. I want to stop smoking, Sensei—I really do. It will help me a great deal once I reclaim my health and regain my control."

"Good! You correct—an addict never free. Your father knew that, you know. That was his conflict between good and evil."

Reality sucks, as I begin once more to weep in Sensei's presence. I cannot argue against the wisdom he has shared with me.

"You ever wonder why I feel special closeness to you, Freedom?"

"No, I never have actually. Why?"

"My son, Ernest, was only thirteen—" Sensei's eyes swell with tears. "Need moment to…."

As Sensei tries to hold back his tears, I say softly, "It's okay, Sensei, you can tell me another time."

"No, I cannot. The moment is here for reason. He was like you when you first entered door. Bullies pestered him— he like boys over girls. I told him I was okay because you need to accept destiny. You must be the one you are, not the one you are not. Unfortunately, the bullies did not see it this way. Instead, they called him names, like what happen to you before you first enter my door."

"You never mentioned your son before now, Sensei."

"…And never will again, Freedom."

"Why not?"

"One afternoon, I expect him to lead class for young people. Ernest was at sixth *kyū* rank, soon to test for fifth *kyū*. He never arrive. Before I could look for him, police arrive at dojo. I knew something bad happen by look in officer's eyes. My world collapse as officer say that Ernest did best he could—two of them in hospital, but Ernest not lucky. My good friend kept me alive somehow for next few months. I wanted to check out—sayonara forever."

"My God, Sensei, I never knew this. I feel terrible."

"No, do not feel terrible, Freedom. Life is what happen to you, and many things we cannot control. The sun sets each night despite my feeling about it. Each night, darkness reminds me of my sorrow. However, while I breathe, I do what I can by helping others…in ways I could not help my son."

"I understand, and I will honour you, your son, and my father. I finally get it."

"I excited to hear that. Here is business card of my friend. You call tomorrow and say I sent you. He will know what to do."

"Thank you, Sensei."

We bow, and I leave. Once again, I leave the dojo feeling like I'm on a natural high. I had forgotten the deep sense of connectedness I felt when I was involved in something more important than myself. Through aikido, Sensei reminds me that in life, we often train for a fight that does not occur the same way that we envision it. Instead, the fight is far deeper than what you actually see.

Chapter 7

FIGHTING LESSON #1:

INITIATING COMBAT

I look at the card Sensei gave me. The name on it is Dr. Robert Yang, psychologist. I phone and he answers.

"Hello, Dr. Yang here."

"Hello, my name is Freedom. Sensei Hiro asked me to call you. I need help to stop smoking now."

"Good. Can you come here today at one p.m.?"

I look at my watch and notice it's already noon. "Yes," I reply, "that works for me. I'll be there in an hour." *Click*. There's no point in giving this a second thought. The sooner I do this, the sooner I can completely focus on other things in my life.

Nothing should surprise me anymore, but as I enter Dr. Yang's office, I find him sitting with his eyes closed, barefoot in a lotus position against the feature wall in front of me. There is no furniture in the room at all. I know better than to say a word when someone is in deep meditation, so I simply sit quietly on the floor until he decides to acknowl-

---

1. Instructions for *BAMM!* is found in Part D. Save reading about this until later.

edge me. After a few minutes, he rouses, unlocks his legs, stands, and greets me.

"Hello, I'm Dr. Yang. You are here to stop smoking, Freedom?"

"Yes, that is correct. Sensei Hiro recommended you very highly."

"I know. I helped him through many difficult challenges in his life. Now as for you, there are two things I want to teach you before we move to the next step. The first is called abdominal breathing. We will do this at the same time so you learn it well. Are you ready?"

"Yes, I am."

"Good. First, focus on making your breathing slow, steady, and rhythmical. Now begin deep breathing, but do *not* hold any of these breaths. Good—it is good to see you still know how to breathe!"

I'm not sure I appreciate Dr. Yang's sarcasm, and I'm not sure why I feel the familiar anger growing rapidly inside me. *"Of course I know how to breathe!"* I scream out.

"Freedom, what is wrong with *you?*"

I stumble on his words, doing a backflip in my head this time instead of in reality. Why am I so irritable? What kind of monster have I become? I think hard inside. "Forgive me, Dr. Yang, I don't know the answer to your question."

"You have forgotten your centre, Freedom—your *true* centre, I mean. I will help you find it again. Now place one hand on your stomach. As you inhale, make your stomach rise as much as possible. Let your stomach puff out as you breathe inward. It feels like you are breathing air into your stomach. Do it now…how do you feel?"

"I feel a hundred percent better already!"

"It's that easy! Doing that for a few minutes will help you relax, which in turn will help reduce the craving to smoke. I will now teach you one final technique for today before our next appointment. I call it 'muscle contraction – simultaneous.' Here is what you do. Contract as many muscles as you can at the same time—like this." At this point, Dr. Yang demonstrates the most hideous-looking contortion I have ever seen.

I am doing my best to control my laughter at how ridiculous this looks, but Dr. Yang notices the sides of my mouth curl upwards as he pauses for a moment.

"You find this funny, Freedom?"

"Actually I do, Dr. Yang!" while I begin to laugh like some kind of hyena. We both share a belly laugh for the next few minutes.

"Okay, now back to business. I forgot to teach you one thing—the most important thing. It's a sequence of steps, like the many patterns you have learned in aikido. In the technique called *BAMM!* you will learn to regain your centre whenever a smoking craving appears." After demonstrating this powerful technique,[1] Dr. Yang says, "Ready to try it, Freedom?"

"Okay, here goes." At that point, I take three abdominal breaths, followed by telling myself positive thoughts about being a non-smoker. I then massage my right hand, and after that, I contract all of my muscles at the same time. "Should I say the positive thoughts or affirmations out loud or just to myself, Dr. Yang?" I ask.

"Either way is okay, Freedom. Try both; see which one

work better for you."

"Will do."

"Good. Now the rest of what I want you to do to prepare for quit day is contained in these sheets I give you. Take them home and study. Training is training, Freedom. Do not short change yourself—learn these methods well. It's like being caught in a back alley at night; only training will prepare you adequately. Understand?"

"Yes, Sen— I mean, Dr. Yang. I know this lesson well now."

"I haven't asked you yet, Freedom, but how much do you currently smoke?"

"Usually one and a half packs a day, but more when I'm stressed."

"Okay, then before I see you next, see your family doctor. The right medications will double your success rate without you doing anything else!"

"It sounds good to me, Dr. Yang."

"These medications need to be started seven to ten days before quit day, so I don't want you to set quit date until you have taken the first step."

"You just reminded me of weight gain, Dr. Yang. I love the way babes are checking me out because of my hard-muscled body. What medications will help prevent weight gain?"

"Your physician will tell you about this, Freedom. You are forgetting something very important here, though. I understand you are back in aikido, and exercise is one of the best ways to maintain muscle and keep your weight down, together with a good diet."

"Sounds good, Dr. Yang. I will contact you again immediately after I see my family physician."

"Perfect. It has been a pleasure meeting you, Freedom."

I leave Dr. Yang's office, impressed by his knowledge and his confidence.

Chapter 8

Deeper Healing

I schedule an appointment to see Dr. Michaels a week from today. In the meantime, I content myself with focusing on aikido and on looking for another job. I get hired as a labourer for a construction site, and although the weather is cool right now, I'm thinking that the additional exercise will keep my physique taut and in the summer I will get a great tan. The job begins tomorrow.

I decide to walk barefoot to the dojo despite the coolness in the air. Several people look at me as though I'm mad, but I really don't care what other people think. This is my life, and I will live it the way I want. Nobody is going to tell me what to do.

I arrive at the dojo before the others, so I wipe my feet clean before bowing and taking my place on the mat.

Sensei notices my entrance and he comes over to me to say, "What happen to your shoes, Freedom?"

"I walked here in bare feet, Sensei. My shoes are at home."

"Hmm, so much like rebel. Who does this remind you of?"

I pause for a moment as emotions once more surge within me. I am strong today, however, and I will not cry for anyone, especially not Sensei. "It reminds me a little of my father, I guess."

"Yes, Freedom. As you accept rebel within yourself, you will learn to accept rebel within your father."

Sensei is pushing it this time. I'm not sure how to feel, but I don't like the sensation inside. "But he was a rebel without a cause…." I pause as I realize I started the sentence all wrong. "What I mean is his rebelliousness was harmful. Walking here in bare feet is not harmful to me or anyone else."

"Freedom, I proud of you for walking barefoot because you are correct—it hurt no one. Is this only way you have rebelled?"

"What do you mean, Sensei?" I ask, pretending not to know what he is talking about.

"You know what I mean. Tell me things you not proud of."

"God, do I have to? Can't I just enjoy the class like everyone else without going through Twenty Questions?"

"Freedom, you not just learning self-defense; you learning aikido. Have you forgotten?"

"Sorry—I beg your forgiveness, Sensei. Okay, I have hurt other men, I have been a drunk, and I smoke cigarettes. Is that enough?"

"It enough if it helps you understand. You also been rebel without cause at times."

"Okay, I accept that I have been a senseless rebel too at times."

"Good. Now what that mean in terms of your father?"

"It means I need to accept that I'm no better than my father."

"That is half of equation, Freedom. What is other half?"

"I'm no better and no worse than my father."

"Exactly. If you no better and no worse than father, then what is your relationship to your fellow man and woman?"

"I'm no better or worse than them either."

"You are growing, Freedom. I very proud to see this before my eyes."

Sensei never told me before that he is proud. Before my eyes get too soggy again, I excuse myself and quickly head for the washroom. I lean over the sink while I fill it the best I can without turning on the taps. I don't need to—he struck another chord. I begin thinking about how much I loved my dad. Why did he have to leave me so soon? I try to shake off the tears prematurely, but I have learned that we must complete each step in life before we can truly move on to the next. I pause, reflect, and let myself feel what I need to feel. A warm glow soon fills my heart as a longstanding burden lifts like an albatross that no longer needs to hang around my neck. My composure regained, I now feel ready to begin really learning about aikido and the circle of life and movement.

Chapter 9

FIGHTING LESSON #2:
TAKING THE OFFENSIVE

Like Sensei told me earlier, it's okay to be a rebel in the areas of life that cause no harm to myself or others. Sometimes I like to push boundaries, and I now accept that I learned this valuable lesson from my father. I walk to Dr. Michaels' office in bare feet, and although no one says anything, I certainly get a few weird looks from others in the waiting room.

The nurse escorts me to the examination room and I wait there for not more than ten minutes before the door opens and Dr. Michaels enters.

"Freedom, nice to see you again. How have you been feeling?"

"To tell you the truth, Dr. Michaels, I've been feeling better than I've ever felt. Sensei has helped me recover physically, emotionally, and spiritually."

"I'm pleased to hear this. What brings you in today to

---

2. http://www.pfizer.ca/english/newsroom/press%20releases/default.asp?s=1&releaseID=220

see me?"

"I have decided to quit smoking with help from Dr. Yang, a local psychologist. He told me to book this appointment to discuss medication aids with you. I have a few questions I would like to ask."

"Excellent, Freedom. Your psychologist has given you good advice. I would be pleased to answer your questions."

"Great. Call me a bit vain, but I don't want to gain weight when I quit smoking. Dr. Yang said there are medications that can help. What are these medications?"

"Bupropion—also known as Zyban—helps a great deal, particularly in combination with nicotine replacement therapy. There are five types of nicotine replacement therapies currently available, all without prescription: the nicotine patch, nicotine gum, nicotine lozenges, nicotine inhaler, and nicotine nasal spray."

"Interesting. It just occurred to me—does quitting smoking affect any medications that someone might already be taking on a regular basis?"

"That's a very good question, Freedom, and the answer is yes. If a patient is taking theophylline—for asthma, for example—quitting smoking itself can cause theophylline plasma levels to rise! This means these individuals should talk to their physician before they decide to stop smoking. Smoking cessation can also change the circulating drug levels for those taking insulin, adrenergic agonists and antagonists, flecainide, or tacrine."

"Sorry I asked! I don't recognize any of those medications. Are there any new medications that can help smokers quit?"

"Freedom, I am very impressed by your questions! I

wish more people did their homework before coming to see me. The new drug varenicline is called Chantix in the U.S. and Champix in Canada and has been recently approved. It's a very new drug. Manufacturers such as Pfizer claim it is more effective than bupropion.[2] It helps relieve cravings and withdrawal symptoms, and reduces the enjoyable effects produced by smoking."

"Thank you. I now think I know more than I care to!" I say in jest. We both have chuckle about that. "What would you recommend in my case, Dr. Michaels?"

"How much do you smoke right now?"

"I've been cutting back, but I still average about thirty cigarettes a day."

"Okay, because you are also concerned about weight gain, I will prescribe bupropion, the nicotine patch, and the nicotine inhaler. Only use the inhaler if you feel you cannot control the urge to smoke in some other way. Has Dr. Yang taught you other ways to reduce cravings?"

"Yes, he taught me something he calls *BAMM!* I will try it before I decide if I need to use the inhaler. Thank you so much for your help today."

"The pleasure is all mine. I am extremely pleased that you have decided to quit smoking. This is the best news you can tell your physician!"

As I'm leaving, Dr. Michaels blurts out a final comment, "Freedom, it's great to see you come here in bare feet. The last patient who did this was your father, and I always admired his philosophy of living!"

"Thank you. Take care," I say as I again feel a momentary pause in my composure. Like father, like son—that expression makes sense to me now.

I phone Dr. Yang and he tells me to come back tomorrow at 1 p.m. I ask for a later appointment, as I have already started my construction job, and he replies that 6 p.m. would be okay.

That night, I fall into a deep sleep, allowing my mind to tell me something that is so typical of how the unconscious works. In my dream, I walk down a mysterious tunnel. When I arrive, an angel greets me and asks if I have an appointment.

I say, "Um, if this is heaven, I think I'll take a rain check. I have some unfinished business to attend to. I'm sorry, but heaven needs to wait."

"Are you sure you didn't have an appointment with your father? He is waiting for you."

"My dad…? My dad is here?"

"Are you surprised, Freedom?"

"No, sorry, it's not that…it's…it's just that I miss him so much right now. I need him."

"Then enter. I will take you to him right now."

The tears running down my face now are tears of joy. I can't wait to see him.... "Dr. Yang, what are you doing here?" Before he can answer, I realize he is levitating on a cloud of smoke, about three feet off the ground. I am confused, disappointed, and sad. Where is my father? *Where is my father?!* I wake, sweating, not sure if what I experienced was a curse or a blessing.

I feel off all day—strangely confused, disappointed, and sad. I do my best to shake the smokescreen, and thankfully I succeed before I see Dr. Yang.

Chapter 10
FIGHTING LESSON #3: UP IN SMOKE

I arrive at 6 p.m. and Dr. Yang is sitting on the floor, waiting for me. He really is the most unusual psychologist! I've never met a professional who sits in bare feet and has no office furniture. I have to admit, however, that I like his casual attitude. He and Sensei both remind me a little of my father.

"You saw your doctor, Freedom?"

"Yes, and he prescribed Bupropion, the patch, and the inhaler. I picked them up from my pharmacy last night after work."

"Excellent. Now today is April twentieth, and ten days from now is April thirtieth. Does April thirtieth make sense for quit day?"

"Absolutely. I'm very determined to quit now and there is no point in waiting beyond the minimum."

"Very good. I learned many years ago that the best time to quit is when you are ready to quit. You are ready, so April thirtieth now becomes quit day.

"Excellent!" I say feeling a little fear but mostly excitement. Sensei taught me long ago that fear is not a useful emotion when it comes to making important life decisions. Most of us are afraid of change, but so what? We still need to move forward in life instead of staying stuck.

Dr. Yang comes back with, "Perfect. On April thirtieth, which is a Thursday, you come to see me first thing in the morning before you begin work—be here at seven a.m. I will then teach you what to do. Between now and then, continue all of the steps I told you during our first session."

I have actually been doing so faithfully since I made the decision to quit. Once quit day arrives, I also won't drink alcohol for the first two weeks and I will destroy my last pack of cigarettes when I see Dr. Yang again on April thirtieth. I have also practiced the *BAMM!* technique on a daily basis, as I know I will be better able to remember to use it by making it a habit.

Dr. Yang then blurts out, "Go now."

Taken aback by his abruptness, I bow instinctually before I say, "Bye for now." As I depart, I wonder how Dr. Yang ever got into this line of work. He is an odd person, like many people who inhabit the earth. Maybe *I* am the odd one? Hmm.

Chapter 11

FIGHTING LESSON #4:

GOING FOR THE JUGULAR

Besides the steps I'm taking to stop smoking, let me update you with how I'm progressing with aikido. It's a bit like riding a bike, you know—once you learn it, you never really forget how to do it. All that happens is you get a bit rusty. Now that I'm dedicating myself to getting fit again and practicing proper aikido methods, my training is going really well. This martial art, which is probably not unlike other ones, is about becoming self-controlled and self-disciplined. I'm learning that these principles go far beyond the art of aikido: they are about general life management. If you're disciplined in one area of your life but you completely let yourself go in another, then what does that say and what does that mean? What it means to me is that I need to get back on track in the area that is out of control. If I don't rule my life, someone else will!

I have to be the master of my own fate. Otherwise, I become some kind of victim, and in retrospect, I think that's what happened when I surrendered myself to joining the gang. I hate to admit it, but I was desperate to belong. The paradox is—or, rather, *was*—I *already* belonged! Sensei and his aikido family had already made a home for me. My parents had also made a home for me, but I rejected that because I needed to rebel. Why? I don't really know why, except I have learned that we block a lot of things out—the real reasons why we do things, for example.

Why did I start smoking? Because I didn't want to risk not belonging to a gang. I know now, however, that it was really stupid. If the gang didn't respect me for who I was already, what was the point of becoming more like them and less like me? That's like entering into a relationship where one tries to change the other. Forget it! I am who I am, and you are who you are. If we meet each other, several options become possible, but they come down to whether we like each other or not. If we don't, so what? If we do, maybe we will form a friendship or something sexual, or something that combines both. Either way, I've learned to never stop being who I am, and who I am was never meant to be under someone else's control, or even worse: under a substance's control.

What substance is going to control me? Fuck that—no substance is going to tell me what I can and cannot do. I'm beginning to understand. Nicotine is a highly addictive drug, and being an addict is no way to live.

The weather is a bit chillier on April thirtieth, but I nonetheless decide to walk to Dr. Yang's in bare feet. Why? Because I can—that's why. If I go through life without enjoying full expression of my senses and my ability to breathe free, then I am losing, not winning. I still like to win, by the way. It's just that most fights aren't worth fighting, but this one is! Thanks to Sensei, I know the real enemy, and it doesn't lurk behind some bush in a seedy park. Those people are disturbed, and neutralizing their attacks is easy. No, the real attack comes from the nemesis within. That is the enemy that must be defeated.

In deep introspection, you can completely lose yourself, and by the time I arrive at Dr. Yang's office, my feet are wet and chilled to the bone. They actually hurt, but hurting isn't the same thing as suffering. I'm not suffering, because I'm the one who freely chose to walk barefoot, and I would never replace the exhilaration of free choice with the suffering from a comfort I didn't ask for. It would be like having a billowy soft bed when you're looking forward to sleeping on a firm mattress. Quitting smoking for me is first about making a free choice to quit. Second, I know that by quitting I will regain even more free choice. Consequently, I feel exhilarated to know that I'm about to quit smoking.

Dr. Yang greets me as I enter. "Did you bring the last of your cigarettes and your cigarette package with you, Freedom?"

"Yes, here they are," I reply as I pull the pack out from my jacket.

"Very good. Now rip up the cigarettes into tiny pieces and discard them here. Then do the same with the cigarette package itself. Now you are ready to defeat the enemy."

For the next hour, Dr. Yang instructs me like a master artist, painting the landscape for me of what I should do for the next two weeks, and for the weeks following. The approach is so logical and thorough that I already know that I too can be above the smoke instead of inside it. I *am* ready to fight or do whatever it takes. Nothing can stop me from achieving my goals—nothing.

"That pretty well wraps it up. Do you have any questions, Freedom?"

"No, I don't. In a nutshell, it looks like I need to focus on my thoughts, feelings, and behaviours as they relate to smoking. Is that it, Dr. Yang?"

"Yes, you are learning well. Know that the first three days are often the most difficult, and that almost all withdrawal symptoms have lost their fight after ten days. Your job is to stay committed, continue taking your medications as prescribed, and use all of the techniques I have taught you. Okay?"

"Yes, I understand."

"Excellent. You are in aikido as I was once. Fight the fights that are worth fighting for, and walk away from the rest whenever possible. *This* one is worth the fight and then some. You will soon discover how powerless the enemy is over the strength of your mind and commitment. In fact, you cannot be defeated. I don't need to see you again unless you desire it."

"Thank you so much for your help, Dr. Yang." I bow before I take leave. Without hesitation, Dr. Yang does the same in return.

Chapter 12

FIGHTING LESSON #5:

KICKING THE CRAP OUT OF CIGARETTES

I decided to read the pamphlet about smoking cessation that was given to me when I was discharged from the hospital. Did you know that between twenty and forty-five percent of smokers don't experience withdrawal symptoms when they quit? This includes some heavy smokers! Well, I'm not getting off quite that easy. However, even when my urges to smoke are strong, I can overcome them most of the time using the *BAMM!* technique. I have used the nicotine inhaler three times over the past week too, but each time I thought that I didn't *really* need it. I mostly wanted to know what effect it would have, and without question, it has helped.

It's now two weeks after quit day, and it hasn't been bad at all. Yeah, I've faced some strong urges at times, but really, it's not the first time in my life I have faced hurdles. As I think about all that I have ever encountered, quitting smoking is easy compared to most of life's adversities. Just getting through adolescence relatively unscathed was harder than this. Keeping down a steady job is harder than this—even now! Construction is hard work, but one consolation is knowing how good the exercise is for my body.

From what I can gather, most people struggle with some aspect of their career. Things don't always go right in life, or go easy for that matter. Compared to other challenges, this one is actually easy! Believe me when I tell you this: *quitting smoking is actually easy* when you've done all the preparatory steps and followed through with good sage advice, from Dr. Yang in my case.

I could belabour what my experience of quitting has been like, including some of the difficult moments and times that felt like crises, but what would be the point? What *is* simply *is*. Part of growing is accepting the things you cannot change. Each one of us will experience our processes of change differently. The wisdom of Dr. Yang is that whatever quitting now looks like, this too is but a moment in time and will soon pass.

I can't wait to tell Sensei about my progress. I go into the dojo as usual and this time yell out, "Oh, Sensei! I have something to tell you!"

"Freedom, you must *never* call me that again!" Sensei looks dismayed and angered at my greeting.

Confused is the least of what I feel. "What do you mean? I don't understand!"

"Freedom, the only one who can take the name of 'Oh Sensei' is the founder of aikido. It is clear from your reaction that you did not know this. All is forgiven."

"My sincerest apologies, Sensei. I didn't mean it the way it sounded. I do know this, but it just came out wrong.

It's like when I called out 'Hi, Jack!' to my friend at the airport. I didn't realize I screwed up until I was arrested and detained by airport security. Wrong choice of words, that's all!"

"I understand, Freedom. What you want to tell me?"

"I just wanted to say that I am doing really well with quitting smoking. My resolve to never smoke again grows stronger each day, every day—my resolve just keeps getting stronger."

"I knew this would be so. It was important for you to know this yourself. Now I tell you next month is test...*the* test. You understand?"

"Oh my God, yes, of course I understand! Are you sure?"

Sensei does not answer and instead walks away to begin teaching the class. My heart is beating so fast that I can hardly stay focused on today's instruction.

A month in an adult's life is nothing and the time passes while you do whatever you do during that month. What I know for sure is that this next month, I walk tall as a non-smoker—and every month that follows. Every breath of air seems more precious now, like the feeling you have knowing that spring is only a heartbeat away.

The month does pass like yesterday didn't happen, and it seems my next moment of real awareness unfolds as I stand centred in the dojo. Now as time slows down, transforming minutes into hours, four black belts attack at the same time. I stay completely focused on my goal, and as they lunge, I neutralize each and every one of them, efficiently taking care not to hurt them as I completely redirect their *ki* (i.e., the force of their attack) toward the mat. Before long, they all stand up, bow, and reposition themselves back to a seated posture near Sensei.

Then from behind my line of vision, I feel someone's presence and I turn around barely in time to find a knife-bearing black belt assailant. I grab his arm, lock it behind his back, and exert pressure on his wrist until the knife falls and he collapses for a moment to relieve the discomfort in his wrist. I assume a natural defensive posture, waiting for my assailant to make his next move. He then comes at me with a flurry of varied attacks, both armed and unarmed. One after another, I redirect his *ki*, until the minutes-like-hours pass.

I notice Sensei is gone, only to reappear in minutes, carrying something I have respected since the day I stepped into his dojo. All black belts now rise and bow toward me. I do the same in return while Sensei hands me my *hakama*, which are aikido pants. Then, he passes me my belt—my *black belt!* Oh my God, I just received my black belt!

Like a karate chop breaking through many pieces of wood, denial is shattered once more, and I feel more naked standing there than I ever felt on Wreck Beach during my growing years. As I take the belt from Sensei, I feel a psychosomatic collapse begin as I fall to my knees and begin crying uncontrollably.

After a few minutes of gut-wrenching sobbing, Sensei shouts, "Congratulations, Freedom! Take moment to breathe and regain composure. Your lesson only beginning."

I now know what he means by this comment. The first *dan* is only the first *dan.* As I continue to train, I will continue to advance in the martial art. Who knows how far it will take me? Or, more accurately, who knows how far I will take it?

It is now 9 p.m. and I leave my test to celebrate at Eddy's pub. Don't freak out—my drinking is once more controlled and I'll only stay for one or two before I head home. I actually mean it this time! You don't always know what you will encounter, however, before you get to your destination. Sometimes the road is rockier than you expect, but, nonetheless, you still have to face it head on with the dignity and respect you deserve.

This time, it's someone else's dignity, respect, and well-being that is at stake. As I make my way to Eddy's and approach the bar I used to frequent, I notice someone getting the living crap kicked out of him by three thugs. One of them is just drawing a knife as I enter the scene. Without thinking, I first make a motion as though I am going to punch the knife wielder in the gut. He automatically reacts by moving his arm down to protect himself while I simultaneously lock his arm and begin bending his wrist backwards hard. Once he drops the knife, I then move him away from the pack of wolves and flip him onto his back through continuing wrist manipulation. Everything is moving very fast and I really don't have time to process my own shock in realizing that the assailants are none other than Mike, Shane, and Cory.

Mike and Cory don't recognize me yet as they move off the intended victim and direct their energies at me. Big mistake! I refocus their energies back on themselves and they both end up rather beat-up by the end of it. Shane has re-entered the picture as well while Mike and Cory are hurting themselves, and as he lunges toward me, I circle around the two I'm neutralizing so that Shane's attack connects with them instead. An outside observer would think the whole episode looks like something out of *The Three Stooges* as they continue to unintentionally clobber each other.

With the attack being over, the victim shakes my hand and our mouths drop as my recognition ignites his. Our facial shock only shifts for a moment before returning to the composed gaze of gratitude reminiscent of minutes earlier. The small butterfly tattoo above his wrist is unmistakable. It's Rex.

Within minutes, the police arrive on an already peaceful scene with me and Rex overlooking the old gang sprawled on the pavement. After over an hour of questioning, we are free to leave while the cops shove the three stooges into a paddy wagon.

We are both thankful, Rex for his life and me for mine. Perhaps now I have shaken the bad karma created by my earlier transgressions. Usually what goes around does come around, and this time, I can leave the scene with respect and dignity intact. Before he leaves, he says to me, "Thank you for saving my life. You have changed, and I'm truly struck by your peaceful aura. It reminds me of the hippies I once knew when I was younger."

"My parents taught me well. Good day to you." We part ways, as our journey together has ended.

For the next several months, I continue my journey of becoming one with the universe while breaking increasingly free from the chains of addiction. I gradually realize that the best way to respect the memory of my father is to keep intact the positive lessons about life he taught me, while discarding the other stuff that formed part of his baggage. Sensei taught me that this too is karma. After all, the '60s weren't all bad, and neither were my father's principles of love and peace, nor protesting that which violates these two principles in any way.

Chapter 13

REFLECTIONS OF A MIDDLE-AGED LOG

Well, I've got no slivers, but my rear end is getting a bit sore. I could tell you much more about my life, but that pretty well wraps up the story of my name and my struggles growing up. As I said earlier, more things make sense in my life as a guy in his forties. It took me forever, it seems, to really learn how to love myself. I know some of you out there struggle with the same thing. We didn't all get what we needed growing up. What we did get, however, is something that we can always build on. I like to think of those early years as a foundation instead of as an anchor that cannot be raised.

Our lives are forever shifting, and the only anchor is the one we throw overboard every now and then before we take some time to breathe—and I mean really breathe. I used to think of my name as a curse. Now I realize it's actually the ultimate blessing. My parents gave me freedom and named me accordingly. I *am* free, and there is nothing worth fighting for more than that. I learned that from my dad, and I wish he were here to see how I turned out.

I have now been a non-smoker for twenty years, and

every day, I thank God I quit when I did. Anytime is a good time to quit, of course. It's just you might not realize how good you will feel until you have this behind you! It's easy to forget what health and vitality *really* feel like. Unquestionably, smoking can rob people of their energy, their strength, their charisma, and their courage. It was time for me to reclaim all of that. I know it's *your* time as well.

As I get up to walk the three hundred or so steps to leave the beach via Trail #6, I see a prepubescent boy doing his best to reach me before I begin my ascent. After catching his breath, he bows, and I bow in return.

"Sensei, what are you doing down here?" he asks. "I'm shocked to see you. I'm here with my family. They're sitting over there in the section that some of the regulars call the 'condos.'"

"Don't be shocked, Jonathan. Many have come here long before me, including my own parents. It's nice to see one of my favourite students here actually."

"Thank you for saying that, Sensei. Come—before you leave here, let me introduce you to my parents."

Although I have had enough sun for one day and really do want to leave, I remember what it is like to be a twelve-year-old, and respect, after all, is a two-way street.

"Mom, Dad, this is Sensei! He holds a *hachidan* rank—the eighth *dan*—in aikido! He is the wisest person I know… well, I mean after you guys," he sputters sheepishly.

"It is a great honour to meet you," his father says with great admiration in his voice. "You are transforming our son into a truly remarkable boy. Thank you from the bottom of our hearts!"

"There is no art without students like Jonathan," I reply. "Thank you for allowing him to attend my classes." With that, I shake their hands and bid my farewell. Jonathan bows in front of me, and I reciprocate.

As I head up the steps of Trail #6, I feel as though I am returning to the surface. I am, however, delighted that you allowed me to take you to a deeper level during our time together. I hope that my story has taught you how to breathe freedom, just as I embrace freedom. I breathe freedom today and every day for the rest of my life. I have learned about myself from one incredible master…not just a master of martial arts but, more important, of life itself.

If I am to be free, I have no choice but to breathe freedom. That may sound like an oxymoron, but it's one that doesn't cause any conflict for my own Sensei or for me. His teaching has always been: "Love your enemy, for it is usually nothing more than a creation within your mind, and such a creation becomes part of the karma you must later confront. However, when you are confronted with a *real* enemy, like addiction, *kick the crap out of it* with all of your heart, mind, and soul! Absorb this wisdom you have been taught, and live free forevermore."

THE BREATHE FREEDOM
STOP SMOKING PROGRAM

Introduction to the Breathe Freedom Stop Smoking Program

Important: You must read the first part of the book before beginning this program

I hope you have enjoyed learning about Freedom, a person who began smoking as a teenager due to peer pressure and before learning important life lessons. Furthermore, I hope you now realize you too can quit smoking as he did. However, you don't have to be an aikido expert to quit smoking! More important, you have to become more of yourself and less of whatever influenced you to start smoking in the first place.

Here is what you do before *you* begin the Breathe Freedom program:

1. Set your quit day for no less than ten days after you schedule an appointment with a family physician.
2. Begin practicing abdominal breathing and muscle contraction (simultaneous) (Part A).
3. Write out your reasons for quitting smoking (Part B).

4. Complete the form dealing with trigger situations (Part C).

5. Practice the *BAMM!* technique often before quit day (Part D).

6. Fill in the chart regarding your strategies for dealing with urges (Part D).

7. Carefully review and implement the other preparatory steps (Part E).

8. Learn and practice self-hypnosis (Part F).

9. Ask people you trust to become part of your support team. Use copies of the Support Agreement for this purpose. It clearly lays out the expectations for these people (Part H). This form is also available for download at *www.insomniacpress.com/breathefreedom*.

10. Beginning on quit day: Follow the instructions carefully (Part G).

Now it's your turn to find out how easy it is to *Breathe Freedom!*

The Intrigue of Hypnosis

As you know, the program you are about to embark on to quit smoking is based on five thousand professional references, research that has been conducted mostly by physicians, psychologists, psychological researchers, and medical researchers. *One* aspect of the Breathe Freedom program is the use of suggestion, better known as hetero-hypnosis (when someone else hypnotizes you) and self-hypnosis (when you hypnotize yourself). Since people are often skeptical of hypnosis before they know anything about it, I thought it would be helpful to provide you with some accurate information before you proceed with implementing the program.

First, it's important to realize that all hypnosis is actually self-hypnosis (Johnson, 1979; Napier, 2000; Ruch, 1975), so what professional therapists can help you with is something you can do on your own. However, self-hypnosis has an advantage over hetero-hypnosis: one's use of imagery (that is, one's ability to visualize) is much richer in self-hypnosis (Fromm et al., 1981).

Remaining skeptical about hypnosis is wise, but only because it remains an unregulated practice. In other words, you don't need to belong to a professional association to practice hypnosis. Consequently, there are many charlatans masquerading as "therapists." Genuine therapists, such as psychologists, psychiatrists, and clinical social workers, belong to professional associations that regulate their practices. One of the areas that is carefully regulated is *competence*, meaning that regulated practitioners are not permitted to work outside of their areas of expertise.

Does hypnosis work? The answer is an unequivocal *yes*. But it works better with some people than with others. The key factor is your hypnotic suggestibility, which is your ability to respond to hypnotic suggestion. This is not the same as gullibility—in fact, hypnotic suggestibility is highest in the highly intelligent. Although hypnotic suggestibility can be trained to some extent, it remains, by and large, a trait that remains stable in most people's lives.

It doesn't matter whether you're highly suggestible or not when it comes to quitting smoking. Self-hypnosis is an adjunctive tool, meaning that it supplements everything else you do to quit smoking. In carefully controlled studies, hypnosis has not been more helpful than other smoking cessation methods (the most important which are contained in this book, by the way) for the majority of participants wanting to quit smoking (Green and Lynn, 2000). Having high suggestibility is only important when hypnosis is the *only* tool you are using to quit smoking. If you aren't that suggestible, it just means that the other components of this comprehensive stop smoking program will be more helpful to you.

Given the above, it is not surprising that the American Psychiatric Association, the American Medical Association, the American Psychological Association, the Canadian Medical Association, the Canadian Psychological Association, and most other medical and psychological professional associations throughout the world recognize hypnosis as a valuable therapeutic tool. As Anbar (2006) reported recently in the use of hypnosis for medical conditions:

[Hypnosis] has been reported as a useful part of the treatment of medical issues including asthma, burns, chest pain, child birth, hypertension, irritable bowel syndrome, insomnia, obesity, smoking cessation, stress-related and migraine headaches, and shortness of breath. Hypnosis also helps patients reduce chronic pain and acute pain associated with medical procedures such as surgery. (97)

The American Psychiatric Association publishes *The*

American Journal of Psychiatry, a globally distributed and highly respected professional journal. One article published in 1993 (volume 150, issue 7) reported that of the 226 smokers in one study who partook in a single session of self-hypnosis, twenty-three percent still weren't smoking two years later! That is impressive given that this scientific study involved only one session. Two recent studies where hypnosis was the only method used reported a forty percent success rate after six months, and another found a forty-eight percent success rate after a year.

PsycINFO, a searchable database created by the American Psychological Association, provides ninety-six studies, and the vast majority of these indicate hypnosis-assisted smokers quitting in varying degrees (the search was done by crossing the term "smoking cessation" with "hypnosis" or "hypnotherapy"). In total, PsycINFO contains over nine thousand references including hypnotic interventions, and MedlinePlus, a searchable web resource hosted by the U.S. National Library of Medicine, contains nearly ten thousand.

Overall, hetero-hypnosis and self-hypnosis are respected therapeutic tools within the psychological and medical community and are helpful in assisting people to quit smoking. Now it's time to find out for yourself how easy it is to quit. Turn the page and start breathing your own form of freedom.

References

Anbar, R. D. 2006. Guest editorial: Enhancing the use of hypnosis in medical practice. *American Journal of Clinical Hypnosis* 49(2):97–99.

Fromm, E., et al. 1981. The phenomena and characteristics of self-hypnosis. *International Journal of Clinical and Experimental Hypnosis* 29(3):189–246.

Green, J. P., and Lynn, S. J. 2000. Hypnosis and suggestion-based approaches to smoking cessation: An examination of the evidence. *International Journal of Clinical and Experimental Hypnosis* 48(2):195–224.

Johnson, L. S. 1979. Self-hypnosis: Behavioral and phenomenological comparisons with heterohypnosis. *International Journal of Clinical and Experimental Hypnosis* 27(3):240–64.

Napier, N. J. 1990. *Recreating yourself: Building self-esteem through imaging and self-hypnosis*. New York, NY: Norton.

Ruch, J. C. (1975). Self-hypnosis: The result of heterohypnosis or vice versa? *International Journal of Clinical and Experimental Hypnosis* 23(4):282–304.

Part A

Abdominal Breathing and Muscle Contraction (Simultaneous)

Abdominal Breathing

Do the following, one step at a time:

1. Regulate your normal breathing cycle by making it slow, steady, and rhythmical. When we're anxious, our breathing becomes choppy. The kind of breathing you want to create is where air enters your lungs at the same pace as you exhale it from your lungs.
2. Begin deep breathing. There is no need to hold any of these breaths.
3. Place one hand on your stomach.

When you inhale, make your stomach rise as much as you can. Do this by letting your stomach puff out as you breathe inward. It will feel as though you are breathing air into your stomach. Mostly what is happening is that you are breathing air into both the top and bottom portions of your lungs. We call this abdominal breathing, and it is the most relaxing form of breathing due to the greater amount of oxygen inhaled.

Muscle Contraction (Simultaneous)

If you have a medical condition or physical problem that might prevent you from doing this type of muscle contraction, simply don't do it. Otherwise, do the following:

Contract as many muscles as you can at the same time. This should involve doing the following steps simultaneously:

1. Scrunching your face together.
2. Pulling your shoulders up as high as possible.
3. Tightening your hands into fists and straightening your arms.
4. Flattening your abdomen and making it rigid.
5. Tightening the muscles in your buttocks.
6. Straightening your legs and pressing your heels down.

Hold the muscle tension for twenty seconds, and then relax your muscles for ten seconds, paying attention to the contrast in how your muscles feel. Repeat by tensing again for twenty seconds followed by ten seconds of noticing the contrast.

Part B

My Reasons for Quitting Smoking

Print your reasons for quitting smoking on the list below. You will be asked to keep this list with you at all times for the first two weeks following quit day. It is best to be as specific as possible in creating your list.

1. _____
2. _____
3. _____
4. _____
5. _____
6. _____
7. _____
8. _____
9. _____
10. _____

3 ACE strategies from: Cofta-Woerpel, L., Wright, K. L., and Wetter, D. W. 2007. Smoking cessation 3: Multicomponent interventions. *Behavioral Medicine* 32(4):135–49.

Part C

ASSESSING AND COPING WITH YOUR TRIGGER SITUATIONS

It is important to have a strategy for dealing with situations in which you used to smoke. These are called *trigger situations* because these situations used to be associated with smoking. A useful method[3] is called ACE strategies: **A**void, **C**ope, **E**scape. These stand for:

1. *Avoid* – As your first defense, try to avoid situations, places, and activities that you associate with smoking. If possible, also avoid smoking friends for a while.

2. *Cope* – As your second defense, do your best to cope with smoking urges. A list of these coping methods is listed in the next part, Part D – Overcoming a Desire for a Cigarette.

3. *Escape* – As your third defense, escape the situation or activity if you can't avoid or cope with it. For example, if you are with friends who start drinking and

smoking, leave the situation. You won't need to do this indefinitely, but it is important to do whatever it takes soon after quitting (perhaps for a month or so).

To help you get in touch with your own trigger situations, do the following:

1. Reflect on the times you quit smoking in the past. What triggered smoking again? List the reason in the left column below.
2. What are events, situations, or activities that you strongly associate with smoking? List these in the left column below.
3. Before quit day, pay attention to the events, situations, or activities in which you smoke. Continue listing these in the left column as well.
4. In the right column, write out what your plan is to avoid smoking in each scenario. Remember to pick from the ACE strategies listed above and from Part D.

Event, Situation, or Activity Associated with My Smoking or Past Relapses	Specific ACE Strategies I Plan on Using to Successfully Deal with It
1	
2	
3	
4	
5	
6	
7	
8	
9	
10	

Part D

OVERCOMING THE DESIRE
FOR A CIGARETTE

During the first two weeks, you are struggling not only with a psychological habit, but also with the physical addiction to nicotine. Consequently, having a desire for nicotine is common. You do not need to succumb to this, however. A progressive approach is recommended in overcoming the desire for a cigarette:

Kick the crap out of most urges using Dr. Alderson's *BAMM!* approach. *BAMM!* is an acronym that stands for the first four steps in overcoming an urge to smoke. The steps are:

1. **B** = *Breathe* – Take three deep abdominal breaths, each time telling yourself, "Breathe freedom and relax," as you exhale.

2. **A** = *Affirmations* – Whenever you want a cigarette, a suggestion enters your mind (e.g., "I'd sure like to

have a cigarette," "I have to have a cigarette," "I'll die without a cigarette"). Overcome this thought by telling yourself a positive affirmation, such as:

"I am a non-smoker now, and I'm feeling better every day as a result."

"I am determined not to smoke, and my desire for a cigarette is becoming less and less."

This is also a good time to use one of your own reasons for quitting as a positive affirmation. For example:

"I won't smoke because it's damaging my health."

"I won't smoke because my children would view me as a weak person for continuing this habit."

3. **M = *Massage*** – Massage either the hand you used to smoke with or your ear for a couple of minutes.

4. **M = *Muscle Contraction (Simultaneous)*** – Contract all of your muscles at once. Instructions for doing so are found in Part A.

If *bamming* your urge hasn't conquered it, then it's time to further kick the crap out of it. Do any of the following (these are *not* listed in any particular order). In the table that follows, list the activities you will use if your urges require further intervention. Add these to your trigger strategy found in Part C:

1. NOTE: The following four strategies were found useful in a study of long-term abstainers and late relapsers ("Overcoming the urge to smoke" in

Psychology of Addictive Behaviors): (a) refrain from thinking about cigarettes, (b) think about not wanting to quit again, (c) exercise, and (d) having snacks (preferably healthy ones).

2. (a) drink water, (b) drink fruit juice, (c) take a walk, (d) think of negative consequences, (e) work harder, (f) chew gum, (g) read or write, (h) talk to a friend or family member, (i) engage in a favourite hobby, (j) hold something in your hand, such as a rubber band or squeeze a rubber ball, (k) do something nice for yourself, (l) encourage yourself, (m) take a bath or shower, (n) stretch, (o) doodle, (p) chew on carrot or celery sticks, (q) polish your glasses, (r) play a sport, (s) touch your toes, and (t) do something nice for someone else.

3. Practice any of the forms of self-hypnosis (see Part F) and allow yourself to simply enter a quiet meditative state. You can use self-hypnosis to help accomplish practically any goal.

4. If you have the nicotine inhaler, nicotine nasal spray, nicotine lozenge, or nicotine gum, use as directed.

5. Listen to the recording included with this book. This specially designed recording further unlocks many of the post-hypnotic suggestions contained in the first section of *Breathe, Freedom*. Please visit *www.insomniacpress.com/breathefreedom* to down-

load it for free.

6. Accept the urge, and ride it out like you would "surf a wave." The urge is telling you to feed it nicotine, but your resolve to be an ex-smoker is stronger. Nothing can force you to embrace the enemy.

Your Strategies for Dealing with Urges

Besides *BAMM!* and the ACE strategies from Part C, which of the preceding interventions will you use if you feel the urge to smoke? Also feel free to add some of your own here:

_____

_____

_____

_____

_____

_____

_____

_____

_____

_____

_____

_____

_____

_____

_____

_____

_____

_____

Part E

Before Quit Day

1. ***Obtain Appropriate Medications*** – If you smoke more than ten cigarettes a day, make an appointment with your family physician and let him or her know that you're quitting smoking. Having appropriate medication can double your chances of success. Research indicates that Bupropion SR (also known as Zyban) is most helpful in reducing cravings and urges. Zyban needs to be started seven to ten days before quit day. If you have been subject to major depression in the past, or have found that you often feel depressed when quitting smoking, Zyban will be especially helpful to you (unless contraindicated). Also very helpful are all of the nicotine replacement therapies (i.e., patch, gum, inhaler, nasal spray, and lozenge). A new medication was recently approved for smoking cessation, called Chantix in the U.S. and Champix in Canada (the generic name is varenicline). It reduces smoker's craving and reduces the symptoms of withdrawal. It also needs to be started seven to ten days before quit day.

2. ***Set Your Quit Day*** – Once you have booked your medical appointment, set your quit day for ten days or later than your scheduled appointment time.

3. ***Don't Do Anything Else While Smoking*** – Begin breaking associations between smoking and other activities (note: the next two points are related to this as well). Don't do anything else while smoking from now on; instead, just sit and pay attention to each puff of smoke (e.g., do *not* work, socialize or converse, drink coffee, or drink alcohol while smoking).

4. ***Pair Breathing with Relaxation*** – After you finish a cigarette, take three deep abdominal breaths, each time telling yourself, "Breathe freedom and relax," as you exhale.

5. ***Break Associations*** – Begin to break down the associations between smoking and eating and drinking. Do not let yourself have a cigarette at least ten minutes before eating and at least ten minutes after you have eaten. Furthermore, if you drink coffee, tea, or alcohol, don't let yourself have a cigarette for at least ten minutes before and after drinking the beverage.

6. ***Get Psychologically Prepared*** – Psyche yourself up (i.e., increase your motivation) for the fact that you will be quitting smoking on quit day. Start convincing yourself that this is the most important goal of

your life. One way to do this is to write something such as the following on the inside flap of your cigarette package: **On _____ [quit day], I am going to become a non-smoker. My commitment is growing stronger each day.** Each time you want a cigarette, read this suggestion to yourself *first*. Think about it for a moment or so before you take your cigarette and begin smoking it. Remember to do point #4 above after you *finish* each cigarette.

7. *Change Brands* – Between now and quit day, change the brand of cigarettes that you smoke at least twice, each time picking a brand that has lower nicotine content than your current brand if possible.

8. *Control Your Surroundings* – If you have other smokers at home, ask them not to leave their cigarettes around the house for at least two weeks following quit day. If possible, ask them not to smoke around you either for at least two weeks.

9. *Enlist Support* – Let significant others (i.e., close friends, family, employer) know about your intent to quit smoking, and ask them to provide you with needed support during the initial period. Provide them with a copy of the Breathe Freedom Support Agreement (see Part H) to help facilitate this request. This agreement form is also available for download at *www.insomniacpress.com/breathefreedom.*

10. Complete All Forms – Complete all forms contained in Parts B, C, and D.

11. Practice Assertive Behaviours – Begin to practice saying *no* when people offer you a cigarette. Do so firmly but kindly.

12. Purchase Vitamins – If you don't already take vitamins, purchase a combination of vitamins B and C, commonly referred to as "stress tabs" in most pharmacies. You will want to start taking these for a couple of weeks commencing on quit day.

13. Obtain Glucose Tablets from Pharmacy – Glucose tablets have been shown to reduce urges. Check with your pharmacist about this (note: if you are diabetic, glucose is contraindicated).

14. Get Rid of Ashtrays – Just *before* quit day, get rid of all your ashtrays.

15. Consider Eliminating Alcohol – Seriously consider avoiding alcoholic beverages during the first two weeks, as they are highly associated with relapse.

16. Destroy Your Last Pack of Cigarettes – As a ceremonial gesture, ensure that you have a few cigarettes remaining before you begin quit day. Have a garbage container in front of you while you crumble each remaining cigarette and rip up the package into many pieces. Time to begin quit day!

17. ***Consider Using Self-Hypnosis As a Way to Relax and Focus on Your Goals*** – Self-hypnosis is an excellent and quick method of relaxation and focused attention for working on a goal, whether it be quitting smoking or nearly anything else (e.g., weight control, improved self-esteem). Instructions for using self-hypnosis are found in Part F.

Part F

INSTRUCTIONS FOR SELF-HYPNOSIS

Preliminary Practice

Spend some time practicing the following three components of self-hypnosis separately before moving to the basic induction itself. These three components are:

1. abdominal breathing
2. muscle contraction (simultaneous)
3. relaxing visual imagery

Abdominal Breathing

Do the following, one step at a time:

1. Regulate your normal breathing cycle by making it slow, steady, and rhythmical. When we're anxious, our breathing becomes choppy. The kind of breathing you want to create is where air enters your lungs at the same pace as you exhale from your lungs.
2. Begin deep breathing. There is no need to hold any of these breaths.
3. Place one hand on your stomach.

When you inhale, make your stomach rise as much as you can. You do this by letting your stomach puff out as you breathe inward. It will feel as though you are breathing air into your stomach. Mostly what is happening is that you are breathing air into both the top and bottom portions of your lungs. We call this abdominal breathing, and it is the most relaxing form of breathing due to the greater amount of oxygen inhaled.

Muscle Contraction (Simultaneous)

If you have a medical condition or physical problem that might prevent you from doing this type of muscle contraction, simply don't do it. Otherwise, do the following:

Contract as many muscles as you can at the same time. This should involve doing the following steps simultaneously:

1. Scrunching your face together.
2. Pulling your shoulders up as high as possible.
3. Tightening your hands into fists and straightening your arms.
4. Flattening your abdomen and making it rigid.
5. Tightening the muscles in your buttocks.
6. Straightening your legs and pressing your heels down.

Hold the muscle tension for twenty seconds, and then relax your muscles for ten seconds, paying attention to the contrast in how your muscles feel. Repeat by tensing again for twenty seconds, followed by ten seconds of noticing the contrast.

Relaxing Visual Imagery

Spend some time relaxing while you create relaxing visual images in your mind. This is the same thing as day-dreaming, except you fully direct the visualizations. The best visual images are detailed, so create as much detail as you can. For example, if you are visualizing a burning candle, see the shape and size of the candle, picture its burning wick, imagine the flame darting about, and see the wax dripping down its sides and falling onto its holder. Also allow as many of your senses into the visual image as possible. For example, imagine hearing people talk to you or other sounds (such as ocean waves), bring in the sense of smell (the ocean air or the scent of melting chocolate), add colour, allow the tactile to develop (in a beach scene, feel the sun's warmth upon your skin and the sand under your feet), and even taste (remember the taste of candy floss).

Here is a sample of relaxing images you could use:

- Lying on a beach
- Hiking through a forest
- Scuba diving
- Feeding birds
- Walking barefoot in a park
- Relaxing in a hot tub

Imagery is best accomplished by introducing as many

senses and details into your visualizations as you can. For example, if you imagine yourself lying on a beach, see the blue sky and blue water (sight), hear the rhythmical sound of ocean waves crashing into shore (sound), feel the warm sand under your hands and feet (touch), smell the fresh ocean air (scent), and recreate the sense of tranquility (feelings). The more vivid your visualization, the more deeply you'll relax.

The Basic Induction Method of Self-Hypnosis

After you've practiced the above three components of self-hypnosis a number of times over a number of occasions, and you feel that you have done each one satisfactorily, it is time to integrate these pieces. There are many different ways to go into self-hypnosis. The advantage of the basic induction method presented here is that it will help you relax your body and mind quickly, thereby allowing you to enter self-hypnosis quickly as well. Once you become proficient in attaining a deep relaxed state following this method, you may wish to shorten the induction further. A simpler induction might include only steps three and four, for example. Let depth be your gauge in deciding whether to shorten the induction eventually.

Follow these instructions:

1. *Get Comfortable* – Get comfortable, preferably lying down with your arms and legs uncrossed.
2. *Contract Your Muscles Simultaneously* – Hold the muscle tension for twenty seconds, then relax your muscles for ten seconds, paying attention to the contrast in how your muscles feel. Repeat by tensing

again for twenty seconds, followed by ten seconds of noticing the contrast.

3. *Fixate Your Eyes* – With your eyes open, stare at a spot slightly behind your normal line of vision so that you feel a mild eye strain. Do not let your gaze drift from that spot.

4. *Engage in Abdominal Breathing Before Closing Your Eyes* – Take in five deep abdominal breaths. Inhale the fifth breath extra deep, and while holding it, count backwards mentally: *five, four, three, two, one*. When you get down to *one*, exhale and close your eyes at the same time.

5. *Create a Relaxing Visual Image* – Spend at least five minutes focusing on a relaxing visual image.

6. *Exit the Self-Hypnotic State* – When you are ready to leave self-hypnosis, first silently tell yourself that you will count to five and that at the count of five, you will come out of self-hypnosis feeling refreshed, relaxed, and confident. Then awaken yourself by counting to five mentally, and say to yourself, "Awake!" Then open your eyes.

That's it! Use the following two methods of self-hypnosis for any goal you set for yourself.

Two Methods of Using Self-Hypnosis

Below are instructions for the two ways of using self-hypnosis: *using verbal suggestions* and *using visual imagery*.

Using Verbal Suggestions

Write a positively worded suggestion on a piece of paper or cardboard. The suggestion should be a one-sentence statement that conveys the intent of your goal. For example, if you wanted to become a calmer individual, you would *not* use the suggestion, "I will try to become less tense each day." There are two reasons for this. First, the word *try* implies the possibility of failure to your subconscious mind. Second, the word *tense* may actually increase your tension. Instead, find a more positive word that means its direct opposite. For example, a positive suggestion is "I will become calmer each day." The word *calmer* suggests the desired outcome.

1. Read the suggestion to yourself five times before entering self-hypnosis. You should read the suggestion slowly, meaningfully, and reflectively so that it becomes the most important thought entering your mind.

2. Place yourself into self-hypnosis using the basic induction method described above and remain there for at least three or four minutes.

3. During these three or four minutes (or longer), you will find that the words in the suggestion begin to enter your mind in an automatic or semi-automatic fashion, although not necessarily in their correct

sequence. If the words are not forthcoming on their own, use as little effort as possible to bring the key words of the suggestion into your mind.

4. Awaken yourself as described in the basic induction method.

Using Visual Imagery

1. Make a list of the various images that you plan to visualize while in self-hypnosis to help you accomplish your goal. In essence, each image selected should reflect the outcome of your goal. For example, to further assist you in quitting smoking, your visual images may include seeing yourself exercising without shortness of breath, taking a holiday with the money you have saved from not smoking, and enjoying your morning coffee without a cigarette. Each image, then, represents the result of being successful at your goal.

2. After you have your list of images prepared, place yourself into self-hypnosis using the basic induction method.

3. Begin to imagine as vividly as you can each of your images. Make each image as real as possible and create a feeling of accomplishment related to each image.

4. After at least three or four minutes of visualization, awaken yourself as described in the basic induction method.

Part G
BEGINNING QUIT DAY

1. ***Do Not Allow Yourself One Puff from a Cigarette—Ever*** – A relapse usually occurs when ex-smokers believe they can handle one puff or just one cigarette. Research has clearly shown that ex-smokers can handle neither. This is one decision you cannot compromise. Smoking is an addiction, and similar to crack cocaine, one puff leads to another. *Vow* to yourself that you will never smoke again, thereby making a promise to the most important person: you!

2. ***Positive Attitude*** – If you learn to view the process of quitting smoking as a positive experience, your mental attitude will assist you greatly in overcoming this habit. For the next two weeks, think of yourself as a king or queen and that you deserve to enjoy yourself immensely for deciding to quit. See the positive in everything you do.

3. ***Most Important Life Goal*** – Think of this as the

most important goal of your life. If you think about it, you may realize that it is without question. The quality of your life is contingent on the quality of your health.

4. ***Reward Yourself Systematically*** – One of the most important reasons why people continue smoking is that they find it rewarding in a certain way. Perhaps you feel it helps you relax or gives you a temporary "lift." The message to your subconscious mind has been: "Smoking is pleasurable and good." That message is a half-truth if not an outright lie. Find other ways to reward yourself. Now that you have decided to quit smoking, it's important that you give your subconscious mind a different message. You accomplish this by rewarding yourself daily for not smoking. At the simplest level, this is done by praising yourself repeatedly throughout the day and by concentrating on a feeling of accomplishment and achievement. It's also helpful to give yourself tangible or concrete rewards, such as enjoying a warm bath, spending time with a loved one, or buying some new clothes.

5. ***Dealing with Urges and Trigger Situations*** – Remember to refer to and use the strategies you came up with earlier in Parts C and D.

6. ***Concentrate on Fresh Clean Breath*** – Use mouthwash twice a day and concentrate for a few moments

on the fresh clean breath it gives you.

7. *Positive Affirmations* – Write down one of the following suggestions on a piece of paper or cardboard
when you're at home. Make it into a poster for yourself. Read it five times before you fall asleep and
five times when you awaken. Read it slowly, meaningfully, and reflectively. Concentrate on what it
means to you and create a feeling of accomplishment.

    a. "I feel a tremendous satisfaction and sense of
freedom in being a non-smoker."

    b. "I am determined to *never* smoke again, and
my powers of control are increasing progres-
sively."

8. *Vitamin Supplements* – Supplement your diet with
vitamins B and C, commonly referred to as "stress
tabs" in most pharmacies.

9. *Short-Term Financial Incentive* – Save the money
you would otherwise spend on cigarettes by putting
it aside somewhere conspicuous before you go to
bed. Spend it on *yourself* after one or two weeks.
Have fun with it—you would have wasted it anyway
as a smoker in a much more harmful way.

10. *Long-Term Financial Incentive* – Establish for
yourself a long-term reward for not smoking. The
best idea is to continue saving the money you used

to spend on cigarettes by placing this daily amount in a piggy bank at home each evening before you go to bed. Save this for six months to a year and then use this money to take a vacation.

11. ***Do Not Envy Smokers!*** – Remember: They are envying you for quitting, just as you used to envy non-smokers before you decided to quit. You are not being deprived of anything; you are reclaiming what you lost since you started smoking: your freedom, your health, your money, your self-confidence, your peace of mind, your energy, etc.

12. ***Accept Negative Feelings As Indicative of Squaring Off against the Enemy*** – You are now engaged in full combat with the enemy (i.e., nicotine), and if you feel a bit more negative or irritable for the first month or so, accept this for what it is. The enemy is launching its pitiful counterattack! Its fight has no substance to it. Remember a principle of aikido here: neutralize the energy of the attack. Do this by redirecting the energy into something useful (see Part D for ideas).

13. ***Practice Self-Hypnosis As Needed*** – Self-hypnosis is an excellent and quick method of relaxation and focused attention for working on a goal, whether that is to quit smoking or nearly anything else (e.g., weight control, improved self-esteem). Instructions for using self-hypnosis are found in Part F.

14. ***Listen to the Recording Provided*** – This is an actual hypnosis session, carefully designed to assist you and activate several of the posthypnotic suggestions contained in the story of Freedom. It's in the author's own voice. Listen to it every day for at least the first two weeks after quitting. Please visit *www.insomniacpress.com/breathefreedom* for the free download.

Part H

THE BREATHE FREEDOM SUPPORT AGREEMENT

I am planning to quit smoking on _____.

I would like your support during the first month of this goal. I don't want you to monitor my smoking or act like a therapist to me. Instead, it will help me if you simply remain positive about what I am doing.

I am taking this attempt very seriously, and I am following a comprehensive smoking cessation program outlined in the book entitled *Breathe, Freedom: A Comprehensive and Hypnotic Approach to Quitting Smoking.*

I will be following this program carefully. I would appreciate receiving help from you in the following ways:

1. Encourage me in my attempt.
2. Listen to me if I need to talk to help get me through a smoking urge.
3. If you smoke, please don't smoke in my presence for a month.
4. Do not offer me cigarettes.

Please avoid doing the following:

1. Taking any kind of responsibility for what I do.
2. Punishing me or being critical of me.
3. Lecturing me or getting on my case if I'm struggling.

_____   _____
My Signature   Your Signature